The Intelligence Handbook

Fourth Edition

A Roadmap for Building an
Intelligence-Led Security Program

Cover and Design by Lucas Clauser
Foreword by Christopher Ahlberg, Ph.D.

CYBEREDGE
P R E S S

The Intelligence Handbook, Fourth Edition

Published by:
CyberEdge Group, LLC
1997 Annapolis Exchange Parkway
Suite 300
Annapolis, MD 21401
(800) 327-8711
www.cyber-edge.com

For general information on CyberEdge Group research and marketing consulting services, or to create a custom *Definitive Guide*™ book for your organization, contact our sales department at 800-327-8711 or info@cyber-edge.com.

ISBN: 978-1-7371618-2-0 (paperback)
ISBN: 978-1-7371618-3-7 (eBook)

Printed in the United States of America.

10 9 8 7 6 5 4 3 2 1

Publisher's Acknowledgements

CyberEdge Group thanks the following individuals for their respective contributions:

Copy Editor: Susan Shuttleworth
Graphic Design: Debbi Stocco
Production Coordinator: Jon Friedman

Acknowledgements

This book's publication was made possible by the Recorded Future personnel who provided their insight and expertise to this fourth edition. Contributors include: **Stas Alforov, Andrei Barysevich, Levi Gundert, Lindsay Kaye, Jason Steer, Chris Ueland, John Wetzel,** and **Ellen Wilson**. Thanks to **Lucas Clauser** for developing the distinctive cover art. We'd like to also thank those who contributed to previous editions of this book.

Foreword by **Dr. Christopher Ahlberg**, co-founder and CEO, Recorded Future.

Table of Contents

Foreword to the Fourth Edition

The global pandemic has accelerated the digitalization of internal, customer, and supply chain operations. Today, everything and everyone is connected, and cybercriminals are taking advantage. Security practitioners, already stretched thin, must now defend a virtually infinite attack surface.

Over the past year, we saw escalating attacks and responses in the form of ransomware gangs halting oil pipelines and food supply chains; civil unrest unfolding around the world and internet use censored and monitored; critical infrastructure being hacked in state-sponsored cyberespionage campaigns; and disinformation campaigns targeting governments and COVID-19 vaccine efforts – to name a few.

Current defense strategies are not working. Defenders must switch to offense. Organizations must move to intelligence-led security programs that anticipate adversaries and their intent, monitor the infrastructure they build, and learn from breached organizations.

At Recorded Future, we believe that intelligence is for everyone. No matter what security role you play, intelligence enables smarter, faster decisions. It's not a separate domain of security. It's the context that empowers you to work smarter, whether you're staffing a SOC, managing vulnerabilities, or making high-level business decisions. To be most effective, intelligence must integrate with the solutions and workflows that you already rely on – and it has to be easy to implement.

In 2020, Recorded Future introduced intelligence modules, tailored to inform specific use cases and outcomes enterprise-wide. In 2021 and early 2022 we extended our enterprise use case coverage by adding three new modules to our Intelligence Platform - Identity Intelligence, Fraud Intelligence, and Attack Surface Intelligence.

Identity is the new perimeter to be validated and defended. We introduced Identity Intelligence to help defenders control access to sensitive data by protecting and verifying user identities, detecting customer identity fraud, and preventing account takeover.

Similarly, it has become increasingly difficult for organizations to identify and prevent payment card fraud before it occurs. Fraud Intelligence helps defenders monitor card portfolio exposure in real-time, identify compromised common points of purchase, and monitor a real-time stream of infected e-commerce domains.

Also, organizations have hundreds or thousands of internet-facing assets that are susceptible to attack, but no visibility into many of them. Attack Surface Intelligence helps them find and protect shadow IT systems, cloud workloads, mobile devices, "forgotten domains," web servers, and IoT devices with IP addresses.

This fourth edition of The Intelligence Handbook provides practical information for developing an intelligence-led security program. We hope you find it to be an informative and useful companion as you integrate intelligence across your security ecosystem.

I am grateful to everyone who has contributed to the development of this Handbook – the users of our platform, our clients, industry experts, and the Recorded Future team.

Christopher Ahlberg, Ph.D.
Co-Founder and CEO
Recorded Future

Introduction

A Complete Picture of Intelligence for Security Teams

You might have heard that intelligence involves collecting data from a wide variety of sources, including the dark web. You may know that it combines that data with insights from security experts, and distills the data and insights into intelligence for IT security professionals. You might work with threat feeds or weekly reports about attacks on the network, or even expert analysis of cyber risks. However, you probably don't know about all the roles and functions that intelligence supports, the number of ways it protects organizations and their assets, and its full potential for reducing risk.

This handbook will give you a complete picture of intelligence and the role it plays in protecting your organization. Section 1 provides an overview of intelligence for security teams and the phases of the intelligence life cycle. Section 2 examines the specific ways that intelligence strengthens several critical security functions and their workflows. Section 3 deals with management and implementation issues, like using intelligence to evaluate risk and justify investments, and how to build an intelligence team.

By the end, you will understand how intelligence amplifies the effectiveness of security teams and security leaders by exposing unknown threats, clarifying priorities, providing data to make better, faster decisions, and driving a common understanding of risk reduction across the organization.

No Longer Just "Threat Intelligence" or "Security Intelligence"

Until recently, the topics discussed in this book were commonly known as "threat intelligence" or "security intelligence."

However, those terms are generally associated with information about threats to traditional IT systems controlled by the organization. This conception of the field is far too narrow.

Innovative threat actors continuously probe for weak points and develop new ways to penetrate or circumvent traditional IT defenses. They steal credentials from trusted third parties and use those to burrow into corporate systems. They harvest personal information from social media platforms to produce convincing phishing campaigns, and create typosquatting websites to impersonate brands and defraud customers. They plot cyberattacks and leverage physical events against remote facilities around the world. They devise attacks that, without prior warning, are undetectable by conventional IT security solutions.

Forward-thinking security experts and IT groups have realized that they need to take the battle to the threat actors by uncovering their methods and disrupting their activities before they attack. This realization has prompted them to expand their intelligence programs to include areas such as third-party risk (exposure through vendors, suppliers, and business partners), brand protection (the ability to detect and resolve security issues that threaten an organization's reputation), geopolitical risk (threats associated with the locations of physical assets and events), fraud intelligence (solutions addressing credit card payment fraud and other fraud related to online transactions), identity intelligence (real-time intelligence about compromised credentials), and more.

Now, we can use "intelligence" to encompass everything that was previously called "threat intelligence" or "security intelligence," as well as the newer areas of the field. That is why the book you're reading right now is titled *The Intelligence Handbook*.

We hope this handbook will empower you to disrupt adversaries, reduce your organization's risk, and serve as a roadmap to help you build an efficient and effective security posture.

Chapters at a Glance

Section 1: What Is Intelligence for Security Teams?

Chapter 1, "What Is Intelligence for Security Teams," outlines the value of intelligence and the characteristics of successful intelligence programs.

Chapter 2, "Types and Sources," discusses the differences between operational and strategic intelligence, as well as the roles of data feeds and the dark web.

Chapter 3, "The Intelligence Life Cycle," examines the phases of the intelligence life cycle and the relationship between tools and human analysts.

Section 2: Applications of Intelligence for Security Teams

Chapter 4, "SecOps Intelligence Part 1: Triage," explores how intelligence provides context for triage and enables security operations teams to make better, faster decisions.

Chapter 5, "SecOps Intelligence Part 2: Response," discusses how intelligence minimizes reactivity in incident response and presents four use cases.

Chapter 6, "Vulnerability Intelligence," examines how intelligence enables practitioners to prioritize vulnerabilities based on true risk to the organization.

Chapter 7, "Threat Intelligence Part 1: Understanding Attackers," explains the value of researching attacker tactics, techniques, and procedures (TTPs).

Chapter 8, "Threat Intelligence Part 2: Risk Analysis," analyzes the value of risk models and how intelligence provides hard data about attack probabilities and costs.

Chapter 9, "Third-Party Intelligence," explores how intelligence is used to assess supply-chain partners and reduce third-party risk.

Chapter 10, "Brand Intelligence," reviews different forms of digital risks to brands and how intelligence empowers security teams to defend their organization's reputation.

Chapter 11, "Geopolitical Intelligence," describes how intelligence provides advanced warning of threats to facilities and physical assets around the world.

Chapter 12, "Fraud Intelligence," provides overviews of several ways intelligence can thwart payment card fraud and other types of fraud related to online transactions.

Chapter 13, "Identity Intelligence," outlines methods for protecting user identities, detecting customer identity fraud, and preventing account takeover.

Chapter 14, "Attack Surface Intelligence," investigates how organizations can discover and protect unknown domains and exposed internet-facing assets.

Chapter 15, " Intelligence for Security Leaders," examines how intelligence enables CISOs, CIO, and other leaders to obtain a holistic view of the cyber risk landscape and make better business decisions.

Chapter 16, "Intelligence for Prioritizing Emerging Threats," highlights three emerging threats every organization should plan for, and how to prioritize them.

Section 3: Creating and Scaling Your Intelligence Program

Chapter 17, "Analytical Frameworks for Intelligence," explains how three leading threat frameworks provide useful structures for thinking about attacks.

Chapter 18, "Intelligence Data Sources and Types: A Framework," presents a framework of intelligence data sources and types that can help organizations anticipate, detect, and respond to a threat.

Chapter 19, "Your Intelligence Journey," provides suggestions on how to start simple and scale up an intelligence program.

Chapter 20, "Developing Your Core Intelligence Team," describes how building a dedicated team takes intelligence to a new level.

Icon Glossary

Tips provide practical advice you may want to apply in your own organization.

When you see this icon, take note, as the related content contains key information that you'll want to remember.

Proceed with caution, because it may prove costly to you and your organization if you don't.

Content associated with this icon is more technical in nature and is intended for IT and security practitioners.

Want to learn more? Follow the corresponding URL to discover additional content online.

Section 1: What Is Intelligence for Security Teams?

Chapter 1

What Is Intelligence for Security Teams?

- Understand why intelligence is important for security teams
- Review characteristics of successful intelligence programs
- Learn who benefits from using intelligence

Visibility Into Threats Before They Strike

Cyber threats come in many forms. Certainly some of them are cybercriminals who attack your network at the firewall. However, they also include threat actors operating on the open and dark web who are trying to gain unauthorized access through your employees and your business partners. Some devastate your brand through social media and external websites without ever touching your network. Malicious or merely careless insiders may also wreak havoc with your data and your reputation.

By the time you see indicators of these threats on your network, it is probably too late. To prevent damage, you need advance warning of threats, accompanied by actionable facts in order to:

☑ Prioritize patching for your most serious vulnerabilities before they are exploited

☑ Detect probes and attacks at the earliest possible moment and with high confidence

☑ Understand the tactics, techniques, and procedures (TTPs) of likely attackers and put effective defenses in place

☑ Identify and correct your business partners' security weaknesses

☑ Detect data leaks and impersonations of your corporate brand

☑ Make wise investments in security to maximize return and minimize risk

Many IT organizations have created intelligence programs to obtain the advance warning and actionable data they need to protect their enterprises and their brands. Figure 1-1 lists metrics that show the dramatic improvement in security and efficiency that an intelligence program provides.

Topline Metrics

Overall more efficient IT security teams
32%

3-year ROI
284%

To payback
4 Months

Security Operational Efficiencies

Less staff time spent compiling security reports
34%

Earlier identification of threats
10x

Faster resolution of security threats
63%

Risk Reduction

22%
More security threats identified before impact

86%
Reduction in unplanned downtime

$1M
Potential penalties/fines per breach avoided

Figure 1-1: An intelligence program can produce dramatic improvements in security, efficiency, and scale. (Source: IDC)

Intelligence: Actionable Facts and Insights

When people speak of intelligence, sometimes they are referring to certain types of facts and insights, and other times to the process that produces them. Let's look at the first case.

More than data or information

Even security professionals sometimes use the words "data," "information," and "intelligence" interchangeably, but the distinctions are important. Figure 1-2 highlights these differences.

Data consists of discrete facts and statistics gathered as the basis for further analysis.

Information is comprised of multiple data points that are combined to answer specific questions.

Intelligence is the output of an analysis of data and information that uncovers patterns and provides vital context to inform decision-making.

Figure 1-2: Distinctions between data, information, and intelligence.

Of course, the details of the data, information, and intelligence differ across political, military, economic, business, and other types of intelligence programs. In the context of intelligence for security teams:

☑ Data is usually just indicators such as IP addresses, URLs, or hashes. Data doesn't tell us much without analysis.

☑ Information answers questions like, "How many times has my organization been mentioned on social media this month?" Although this is a far more useful output than the raw data, it still doesn't directly inform a specific action.

☑ Intelligence is factual insight based on analysis that correlates data and information from across different sources to uncover patterns and add insights. It enables people and systems to make informed decisions and take effective action to prevent breaches, remediate vulnerabilities, improve the organization's security posture, and reduce risk.

Figure 1-3 shows the relationship between data, information, and intelligence.

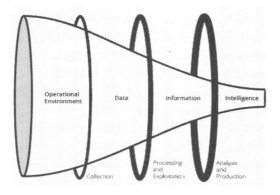

Operational Environment — Data — Information — Intelligence

Collection — Processing and Exploitation — Analysis and Production

Figure 1-3: The relationship between data, information, and intelligence. (Source: U.S. Joint Chiefs of Staff, Joint Publication 2.0, Joint Intelligence)

Implicit in this definition of "intelligence" is the idea that every instance of intelligence is *actionable* for a *specific audience*. That is, intelligence must do two things:

1. Point toward specific decisions or actions
2. Be tailored for easy use by a specific person, group, or system that will use it to make a decision or take an action

Data feeds that are never used and reports that are never read are not intelligence. Neither is information, no matter how accurate or insightful, if it is provided to someone who can't interpret it correctly or isn't in a position to act on it.

Intelligence: The Process

Intelligence also refers to the process by which data and information are collected, analyzed, and disseminated throughout the organization. In industry parlance, this is called tradecraft. The steps in such a process will be discussed in Chapter 3, where we describe the intelligence life cycle. However, it is important to note at the outset that successful intelligence processes have four characteristics.

1. A collaborative process and framework

In many organizations, intelligence efforts are siloed. For example, the security operations (SecOps), fraud prevention, and third-party risk teams may have their own analysts and tools for gathering and analyzing intelligence. They may answer to completely independent reporting chains. This leads to waste, duplication, and an inability to share analysis and intelligence. Silos also make it impossible to assess risk across the organization and to direct security resources where they will have the greatest impact. Intelligence programs need to share a common process and framework, enable broad access to insights and operational workflows, encourage a "big picture" view of risk, and account for the allocation of resources.

2. 360-degree visibility

Because cyber threats may come from anywhere, intelligence programs need visibility within and outside the enterprise, including:

- ☑ Security logs and events from endpoints and network devices
- ☑ External lists from security vendors
- ☑ Community tools such as threat intelligence feeds
- ☑ Community web forums where security researchers share and discuss observation and new findings

☑ Open and closed web forums where attackers advertise new malware and patches and discuss and demonstrate methods for exploiting vulnerabilities

☑ Dark web marketplaces where threat actors advertise exploited machines, bots, and leaked credential databases

☑ Social media accounts where threat actors intimidate and harass victims through open channels

Today, many organizations focus on free or pre-packaged threat data feeds, and are only now becoming aware of the need to scan a broader variety and greater quantity and quality of sources on a regular basis.

3. Extensive automation and integration

Because there is so much data and information to capture, correlate, and process, an intelligence program needs a high degree of automation to reduce manual efforts and produce meaningful results quickly. To add context to initial findings and effectively disseminate intelligence, successful intelligence programs must also integrate with many types of security solutions, such as security dashboards, security information and event management solutions (SIEMs), vulnerability management systems, endpoint and XDR products, firewalls, and security orchestration, automation and response (SOAR) tools.

4. Alignment with the organization and security use cases

Organizations often waste enormous resources capturing and analyzing information that isn't relevant to them. A successful intelligence program needs to determine and document its intelligence needs to ensure that collection and processing activities align with the organization's actual priorities. Alignment also means tailoring the content and format of intelligence to make it easy for people and systems to use.

Who Benefits From Intelligence?

Intelligence is sometimes imagined to be simply a research service for the security operations and incident response teams, or the domain of elite researchers. In reality, it adds value to every security function and to several other teams in an organization.

The middle section of this handbook examines the primary use cases:

- ☑ **Security operations and incident response teams** are routinely overwhelmed by alerts. Intelligence accelerates their alert triage, minimizes false positives, provides context for better decision-making, and empowers them to respond faster.

- ☑ **Vulnerability management teams** often struggle to differentiate between relevant, critical vulnerabilities and those that are less critical to their organization's defense posture. Intelligence delivers context and risk scoring that enables them to reduce downtime while patching the vulnerabilities that really matter first.

- ☑ **Threat analysts** need to understand the motivations and TTPs of threat actors and track security trends for industries, technologies, and regions. Intelligence provides them with deeper and more-expansive knowledge to generate more valuable insights.

- ☑ **Third-party risk programs** need up-to-date information on the security postures of vendors, suppliers, and other third parties that access the organization's systems. Intelligence arms them with an ongoing flow of objective, detailed information about business partners that static vendor questionnaires and traditional procurement methods can't offer.

- ☑ **Brand protection teams** need continuous visibility into unsanctioned web and social media mentions, data leaks, employee impersonations, counterfeit products, typosquatting websites, phishing attacks, and more. Intelligence tools monitor for these across the internet at scale, and streamline takedown and remediation processes.

☑ **Geopolitical risk and physical security teams** rely on advanced warning of attacks, protests, and other threats to assets in locations around the globe. Intelligence programs capture data and "chatter" from multiple sources and filter it to deliver precise intelligence about what's happening in the cities, countries, and regions of interest.

☑ **Fraud prevention teams** use intelligence about online attacks and leaked credentials to detect fraud campaigns, strengthen risk-based authentication, and improve defenses against online fraud.

☑ **Identity and access management teams** can employ intelligence from the dark web to identify compromised credentials of employees and business partners and to prevent people from reusing exposed passwords.

☑ **Security leaders** use intelligence about likely threats and their potential business impact to assess security requirements, quantify risks (ideally in monetary terms), develop mitigation strategies, and prioritize and defend cybersecurity investments to CEOs, CFOs, and board members.

ON THE WEB

For a concise introduction to intelligence and six critical solution areas, read the Recorded Future white paper, "Security Intelligence: Driving Security From Analytics to Action" (https://go.recordedfuture.com/security-intelligence-program).

Chapter 2

Types and Sources

- Differentiate between operational and strategic intelligence
- Appreciate the roles of data feeds, private channels, and the dark web

Two Types of Intelligence

For security teams, there are two types of intelligence: **operational** and **strategic**. These vary in their sources, the audiences they serve, and the formats in which they appear.

The purpose in making this distinction is recognizing that various security teams have different goals and degrees of technical knowledge. As we said earlier, intelligence needs to be actionable — but because the responsibilities of a vulnerability management team differ significantly from those of a CISO, "actionability" has distinct implications for each, and the form and content of the intelligence they'll benefit from the most will vary.

Operational intelligence

Operational intelligence is knowledge about ongoing cyberattacks, events, and campaigns. It provides specialized insights that enable the individuals that use it to understand the nature, intent, and timing of specific attacks as they are occurring.

Operational intelligence is sometimes referred to as **technical security intelligence** or **technical threat intelligence**, because it usually includes technical information about attacks, such as which attack vectors are being used, what vulnerabilities are being exploited, and what command and control domains are being employed by attackers. This kind of intelligence is often most useful to personnel directly involved in the defense of an organization, such as system architects, administrators, and security staff.

Threat data feeds are often used to provide context to internal information, such as internal network telemetry events or endpoint detection and response (EDR) events. These feeds usually focus on a single type of threat indicator, such as malware hashes or suspicious domains. As we discuss below, threat data feeds provide data, but that data is not intelligence. It lacks contextual information, such as the fact that an external IP address is a ransomware command and control server.

Operational intelligence is commonly used to guide improvements to existing security controls, generate or improve new rules in a SIEM, improve security processes and playbooks, and speed up incident response. An operational intelligence solution that integrates with data from your network is crucial because it answers urgent questions unique to your organization, such as, "Should this critical vulnerability, which is being actively exploited by threat actors against my industry, be prioritized for patching?"

Strategic intelligence

Strategic intelligence provides a broad overview of an organization's present and future threat landscape. It informs resource decisions by security leadership and within security architecture, application security, and other security development projects. The content is generally risk oriented and presented through reports or briefings.

This kind of intelligence requires human interaction because it takes analytical thought and creativity to forecast future trends, for example to evaluate and test new and emerging adversary TTPs against existing security controls. Pieces of this process may be automated, but a human mind is required to complete the exercise.

Good strategic intelligence must provide insight into the risks associated with certain actions, broad patterns in threat actor tactics and targets, geopolitical events and trends, and similar topics.

Common strategic intelligence sources include:

- ☑ Trends and research reports from security companies
- ☑ Policy documents from nation-states or non-governmental organizations
- ☑ News from local and national media, articles in industry- and subject-specific publications, and input from subject-matter experts

Organizations must set strategic intelligence requirements by asking focused, specific questions. Analysts with expertise outside of typical cybersecurity skills — in particular, a strong understanding of policy, sociopolitical, and business concepts — are needed to gather and interpret strategic intelligence.

DON'T FORGET

Some aspects of the production of strategic intelligence are dramatically sped up by automated collection. Producing effective strategic intelligence takes deep research on massive volumes of data, often across multiple languages. These challenges make initial data collection and processing too difficult to perform manually, even for those rare analysts who possess the right language skills, technical background, and tradecraft. An intelligence solution that automates data collection and processing reduces this burden and enables analysts with various levels of expertise to work more effectively.

The Role of Threat Data Feeds

We mentioned earlier that data is not intelligence, and that threat data feeds often overwhelm analysts already burdened with countless daily alerts and notifications. However, when used correctly, threat data feeds provide valuable raw material for intelligence.

Threat data feeds are real-time streams of data that provide information on potential cyber threats and risks. They're usually lists of simple indicators or artifacts focused on a single area of interest, like suspicious domains, hashes, bad IPs, or malicious code. They provide a quick, real-time look at the threat landscape.

CAUTION

Many feeds are filled with stale data, errors, redundancies, and false positives. The data lacks context. Many organizations find they have pulled in so many feeds that they need additional steps to process the information, usually manual curation in another tool such as a threat intelligence platform (TIP), before they can push the data into production in a SIEM. This problem is compounded when security managers attempt to widen coverage by investing in a staggering number of data feeds, ultimately creating more noise in their environment.

Evaluating Threat Data Feeds

Use these criteria to assess threat data feeds for your organization:

- **Data sources**: Feeds pull their data from all kinds of sources. You should select sources with care and take the time to evaluate the usefulness and noise of each prior to implementing in your environment.

- **Transparency of sources**: Knowing where your data is coming from empowers you to evaluate its relevance and usefulness. Some sources aggregate from other places, so duplication can be an issue if pulling from multiple sources. You should understand how sources process and update this information and how they purge stale data.

- **Percentage of unique data**: Some paid feeds just aggregate data from other feeds, while others do not take care to place common sources of noise, such as RFC 1918 addresses, on their allow list.

- **Periodicity of data**: Data should be collected frequently, and should cover the time period relevant to your organization. Also, it should cover a long enough timespan to support strategic intelligence on long-term trends. Understanding when data ages off the feed is also important.

- **Measurable outcomes**: Being able to track the correlation rate — the percentage of alerts that correspond with your internal telemetry in a given week, month, or quarter — is critical to calculating the measurable outcomes of a particular feed.

Instead of viewing dozens of feeds separately, some organizations use a threat intelligence platform (TIP) that combines them all into a single feed prior to ingestion in a SIEM. While this can address some of the concerns above, such as removal of duplicates and false positives, this process can be resource intensive compared to providing quality data directly to a SIEM.

The Role of Private Channels and the Dark Web

Threat data feeds and publicly available information are not the only external data sources for intelligence data. Vital operational and strategic intelligence on specific attacks, attacker TTPs, political goals of hacktivists and state actors, and other key topics can be gathered by infiltrating or breaking into private channels of communication used by threat groups. These include messaging apps, exclusive forums on the dark web, and other sources.

However, there are barriers to gathering this kind of intelligence:

- ☑ **Access**: Threat groups may communicate over private and encrypted channels, or require prior validation or an invitation from an administrator.

- ☑ **Language**: Activity on many forums is carried out in many languages, and slang and specialized jargon are used regularly

- ☑ **Noise**: High volumes of conversation make it difficult or impossible to manually gather good intelligence from sources like chat rooms and social media.

- ☑ **Obfuscation**: To avoid detection, many threat groups employ obfuscation tactics like using codenames.

- ☑ **Internal policy:** An organization's legal and security leadership may be hesitant to communicate openly with criminal actors, especially when this requires using corporate assets to pay for access to their forums.

Overcoming these barriers requires a large investment in tools and expertise for monitoring private channels — or an intelligence service provider that has already made that investment.

TIP Look for intelligence solutions and services that employ algorithms and analytical processes for automated data collection on a large scale. A solution that uses natural language processing, for example, will be able to gather information from foreign-language sources without needing human expertise to decipher it.

Chapter 3

The Intelligence Life Cycle

In this chapter

- Examine the phases of the intelligence life cycle
- Review sources of intelligence for security teams
- Explore the roles of intelligence tools and human analysts

The Six Phases of the Intelligence Life Cycle

ntelligence is built on analytic techniques honed over several decades by government and military agencies. There are six distinct phases that make up what is called the "intelligence cycle":

1. Direction
2. Collection
3. Processing
4. Analysis
5. Dissemination
6. Feedback

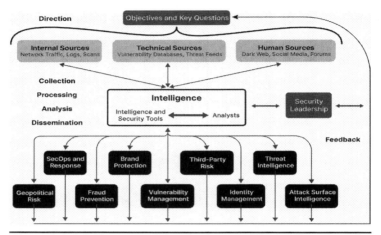

Figure 3-1: Intelligence and the six phases of the intelligence cycle.

Direction

The direction phase of the intelligence life cycle is when you set the goals for your intelligence program. This involves understanding and articulating:

- ☑ The information assets and business processes that need to be protected
- ☑ The potential impacts of losing those assets or interrupting those processes
- ☑ The types of intelligence that your organization requires to protect assets and respond to threats
- ☑ The priorities about what you need to protect

Once high-level intelligence needs are determined, an organization is able to formulate questions that channel the need for information into discrete requirements. For example, if a goal is to understand likely adversaries, one logical question would be, "Which threat actors on underground forums are actively soliciting data concerning our organization?"

Collection

Collection is the process of gathering information to address the most important intelligence requirements. It can occur organically through a variety of means, including:

- ☑ Pulling metadata and logs from internal networks and security devices
- ☑ Subscribing to threat data feeds from industry organizations and cybersecurity vendors
- ☑ Conducting conversations and targeted interviews with knowledgeable sources
- ☑ Scanning news websites and blogs
- ☑ Scanning social media platforms
- ☑ Scraping and harvesting websites and forums
- ☑ Infiltrating closed sources, such as dark web forums

The data collected typically will be a combination of finished information, such as intelligence reports from security experts and vendors, and raw data, like malware signatures or leaked credentials on a paste site.

Intelligence Sources

Technical sources: Technical data sources can be publicly available, such as URLscan.io, and can be ingested through an API. Technical sources generally provide structured data that can be integrated with existing security technologies, but may contain a high proportion of false positives and outdated results.

Media (e.g., security websites, vendor research): These sources often provide useful information about emerging threats, but they are hard to connect with technical indicators to measure risk.

Social media: Social channels offer huge amounts of valuable data, but it comes at a price. Most data from social media is not relevant to security. False positives and misinformation are rampant, so a tremendous amount of cross-referencing with other sources is required to determine which insights are usable.

Threat actor forums: Specifically designed to host discussions about adversary tools and techniques, these forums offer some of the most actionable insights available anywhere. Once again, however, analysis and cross-referencing are essential to determine what is truly valuable.

DON'T FORGET You need multiple sources of intelligence to form a complete picture of potential and actual threats. As shown in Figure 3-1, these include:

- ☑ **Internal sources** like firewall and router logs, network packet capture tools, and vulnerability scans
- ☑ **Technical sources** such as malware repositories and known C2 scanners
- ☑ **Human sources** including traditional and social media, cybersecurity forums and blogs, and dark web forums

Missing any one of these may slow down investigations and cause gaps in remediation.

TIP Automate! Analysts should spend as little time as possible collecting data, and as much time as possible evaluating and communicating threat information.

Processing

Processing is the transformation of collected information into a format usable by the organization. Almost all raw data collected needs to be processed in some manner, whether by humans or machines.

Different collection methods often require different means of processing. Human reports may need to be correlated and ranked, deconflicted, and checked. An example might be extracting IP addresses from a security vendor's report and adding them to a CSV file for importing to a SIEM. In a more technical area, processing might involve extracting indicators from an email, enriching them with other information, and then communicating with ticketing and endpoint protection tools for system remediation.

TIP Automate more! The right tools will enable you to automate most processing workflows and collection processes. For example, a security event might flag a suspicious indicator of compromise (IOC), then conduct a sequence of checks to bring context to the IOC. This saves the analyst valuable time that would otherwise need to be spent performing those checks manually.

ON THE WEB

To learn more about how automation enhances intelligence, read the short Recorded Future e-book, "Beyond SOAR: 5 Ways to Automate Security With Intelligence" (https://go.recordedfuture.com/automation).

Analysis

Analysis is the process of turning information into intelligence to inform decisions. Depending on the circumstances, these decisions might involve whether to investigate a potential threat, what actions to take immediately to block an attack, how to strengthen security controls, or how much investment in additional security resources is justified. Analysis is generally performed either by a human or a very sophisticated algorithm.

DON'T FORGET

Analysts must have a clear understanding of who is going to be using their intelligence and what decisions those people make. The intelligence they deliver needs to be perceived as actionable, not as academic. Most of this book is devoted to giving you a clear picture of exactly how intelligence improves decision-making and actions in different areas of security.

The form in which the information is presented is especially important. It is useless and wasteful to collect and process information only to deliver it in a form that can't be understood and used by the decision maker.

For example, if you want to communicate with non-technical leaders, your report should:

- ☑ Be concise (a one-page memo or a handful of slides)
- ☑ Avoid confusing and overly technical terms and jargon
- ☑ Articulate the issues in business terms (such as direct and indirect costs and impact on reputation)
- ☑ Include a recommended course of action

Some intelligence may need to be delivered in a variety of formats for different audiences, like a live video feed and a written brief. Not all intelligence needs to be digested via a formal report. Successful intelligence teams provide continual technical reporting to other security teams with external context around IOCs, malware, threat actors, vulnerabilities, and threat trends.

Dissemination

Dissemination involves getting the finished intelligence output to the places it needs to go.

As illustrated in Figure 3-1, most security organizations have multiple teams plus security leaders who benefit from intelligence. For each of these audiences, you need to ask:

- ☑ What intelligence do they need, and how does external information best support their activities?
- ☑ How should the intelligence be selected and organized to make it easily understandable and actionable for that audience?
- ☑ How often should we provide updates and other information?
- ☑ Through what media (emails, newsletters, web forums, documents, slides, oral presentations) should the intelligence be disseminated?
- ☑ How should we follow up if they have questions?

Feedback

Regular input is required to understand the requirements of each group and make adjustments as their requirements and priorities change. That input is gathered in the feedback phase. It is critically important to understand your overall intelligence priorities and the requirements of your "customers" — the security teams that consume the intelligence. Their needs guide all phases of the life cycle and tell you:

- ☑ What types of data to collect
- ☑ How to process and enrich the data to turn it into useful information
- ☑ How to analyze the information and present it as actionable intelligence

To whom each type of intelligence must be disseminated, how quickly it needs to be disseminated, and how fast to respond to questions

TIP For every "customer" team, establish channels for both fast, informal feedback (such as an email address, an internal forum, or a team collaboration tool), and a formal, structured process (such as an online survey or a quarterly face-to-face meeting). The informal channel enables you to react and adjust immediately, while the structured process ensures that you get input from everyone and are able to track your progress over time.

Tools and People

Tools are essential to automating the collection, processing, and dissemination steps in the intelligence life cycle — and to supporting and accelerating analysis. Without the right tools, analysts will spend all their time on the mechanical aspects of these tasks and never have time for analysis.

Most mature intelligence groups leverage two types of tools:

 An intelligence solution designed to collect, process, and analyze all types of threat data from internal, technical, and human sources

 Existing security tools, such as SIEMs and security analytics, which collect and correlate security events and log data

Human analysts are equally important — if not more important. You can't rely on tools to interview security experts and probe closed dark web forums. Also, you need people to analyze and synthesize intelligence for the security teams and managers who will consume it.

The analysts do not need to belong to a central, elite intelligence department. Someone does need to take an organization-wide view of the intelligence function, make decisions about resources and priorities, and track progress, but success is achievable under a variety of organizational structures. You could have a central group with dedicated intelligence analysts, or a small group inside the security operations and incident response organization. Alternatively, members of the different security groups may be responsible for analyzing intelligence for their direct colleagues.

In Chapter 19, we discuss how the organizational structure often evolves as the intelligence function matures, and Chapter 20 provides advice on how to organize a core intelligence team.

Section 2: Applications of Intelligence for Security Teams

Chapter 4

SecOps Intelligence
Part 1 – Triage

In this chapter

- See how "alert fatigue" risks undoing the good work of SecOps teams
- Understand the value of context for improving triage
- Learn how intelligence reduces wasted time and improves triage decisions

Triage is a critical but exhausting job for security operations teams. They find themselves held hostage to the huge volumes of alerts generated by the networks they monitor. According to the Ponemon "Cost of Malware Containment" report, security teams can expect to log nearly 17,000 malware alerts in a typical week. That's more than 100 alerts per hour for a team that operates 24/7. And those are only the alerts from malware incidents. To put these figures in perspective, all these alerts can force security teams to spend more 21,000 man-hours each year chasing down false positives. That's 2,625 standard eight-hour shifts needed just to distinguish bad alerts from good ones.

Let's examine how intelligence mitigates this overload by filtering out false alarms, speeding up analysis of alerts, and providing context to make better triage decisions.

Responsibilities of the SecOps Team

On paper, the responsibilities of the SecOps team seem simple:

- ☑ Monitor for potential threats
- ☑ Detect suspicious network activity
- ☑ Contain active threats
- ☑ Remediate threats using available technology

When a suspicious event is detected, the SecOps team investigates it, then works with other security teams to reduce the impact and severity of the attack. Think of the roles and responsibilities of SecOps as similar to those of emergency services teams responding to 911 calls, as shown in Figure 4-1.

Stage	Role	Responsibilities
Triage	Operator (911 Center) Security Analyst (SOC)	Determine the relevance and urgency of each incoming alert. Decide if the alert is legitimate and should be escalated.
First Response	First Responder (911) Incident Responder (SOC)	Determine the scope of the incident. Identify affected and vulnerable systems. Recommend actions to contain the effects.
Investigation	Detective (911) Threat Hunter (SOC)	Determine root causes and weaknesses in defenses. Recommend actions to prevent recurrences.

Figure 4-1: The roles and responsibilities of emergency services teams and SecOps teams are similar.

The Overwhelming Volume of Alerts

Over the past several years, most organizations have added new types of threat detection technologies to their networks. Each of these tools sounds an alarm when it sees anomalous or suspicious behavior. In combination, these tools create a cacophony of security alerts. SecOps analysts are simply unable to review, prioritize, and investigate all of these alerts on their own. All too often they ignore alerts, chase false positives, and make mistakes because of alert fatigue.

Research confirms the magnitude of this challenge. In its "2020 State of the SOC" report, SIEM provider Exabeam revealed that security operations centers (SOCs) are understaffed according to 39 percent of professionals who work in them — and of those, 50 percent think they need at least six additional employees. Additionally, Cisco's "2020 CISO Benchmark Study" found that organizations can investigate only 48 percent of the security alerts they receive on a given day, and of those investigated alerts, only 26 percent are deemed legitimate (Figure 4-2).

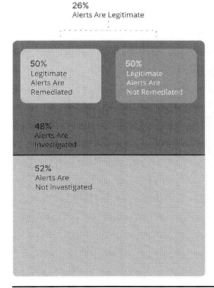

Figure 4-2: Many threat alerts are not investigated or remediated. (Source: Cisco)

Context Is King

SecOps intelligence is used specifically to support triage by enriching internal alerts with the external information and context necessary to make risk-based decisions. Context is critical for rapid triage, and also very important for scoping and containing incidents.

Triage requires lots of context

A huge part of an average SecOps analyst's day is spent responding to alerts generated by internal security systems, such as SIEM or endpoint detection and response (EDR) technologies. Sources of internal data are vital in identifying potentially malicious network activity or a data breach.

Unfortunately, this data is often difficult to interpret in isolation. Determining if an alert is relevant and urgent requires gathering related information (context) from a wide variety of internal system logs, network devices, and security tools (Figure 4-3), and from external threat databases. Searching all of these threat data sources for context around each alert is hugely time consuming.

Key Aspects		Security Monitoring Requirement
	Business Traffic Crossing a Boundary	Traffic exchanges are authorized and conform to security policy. Transport of malicious content and other forms of attack by manipulation of business traffic are detected and alerted.
	Activity at a Boundary	Detect suspect activity indicative of the actions of an attacker attempting to breach the system boundary, or other deviation from normal business behavior.
	Internal Workstation, Server, or Device	Detect changes to device status and configuration from accidental or deliberate acts by a user, or by malware.
	Internal Network Activity	Detect suspicious activity that may indicate attacks by internal users, or external attackers who have penetrated the internal network.
	Network Connections	Prevent unauthorized connections to the network made by remote access, VPN, wireless, or any other transient means of network connection.
	Session Activity By User and Work Station	Detect unauthorized activity and access that is suspicious or violates security policy requirements.
	Alerting on Events	Be able to respond to security incidents in a time frame appropriate to the perceived criticality of the incident.
	Accurate Time in Logs	Be able to correlate event data collected from disparate sources.
	Data Backup Status	Be able to recover from an event that compromises the integrity or availability of information assets.

Figure 4-3: Key aspects of security monitoring and internal sources of context. (Source: UK NCSC)

Use case: Correlating and enriching alerts

An analyst attempting to triage an initial alert without access to enough context is like a person trying to understand a news story after reading just the headline. Even when the analyst has access to external information in the form of threat feeds (Figure 4-4), that information is very hard to assimilate and correlate with other data related to the alert.

2021-09-13 02:46:26	E	63.153.27.53	offline
2021-09-12 21:41:44	E	75.130.100.165	online
2021-09-12 18:54:45	E	71.172.252.50	online
2021-09-12 15:51:16	E	118.189.9.243	offline
2021-09-12 14:11:41	E	31.167.248.50	offline
2021-09-12 08:32:01	E	78.134.74.39	online
2021-09-12 05:03:02	E	42.114.73.81	offline
2021-09-12 04:56:53	E	216.59.200.206	offline
2021-09-11 11:35:10	E	183.82.97.20	offline
2021-09-11 08:59:59	E	128.2.98.139	offline
2021-09-11 08:12:12	E	47.38.231.174	offline
2021-09-11 08:01:28	E	217.36.122.251	offline
2021-09-11 07:45:59	E	107.184.160.132	offline
2021-09-11 06:45:54	E	71.75.206.192	online
2021-09-11 06:43:49	E	123.231.21.141	offline
2021-09-11 05:54:51	E	189.222.75.8	offline
2021-09-11 05:54:51	E	189.211.177.113	offline
2021-09-11 05:54:51	E	92.27.115.15	offline
2021-09-11 05:54:51	E	207.107.101.210	offline
2021-09-11 05:31:45	E	185.97.32.6	online

Figure 4-4: It is very difficult to find relevant information in a raw threat feed and correlate it with other data related to an alert.

SecOps intelligence completely transforms this situation. It has the capability to automatically surface real-time threat insights and correlate it with alerts, as illustrated in Figure 4-5. The context provided might include first and most recent references to a piece of malware or a suspicious IP address, the number of sightings, associations with attack types and specific threat actors, and descriptions of the behavior of the malware or the uses of the IP address (say, as part of a botnet).

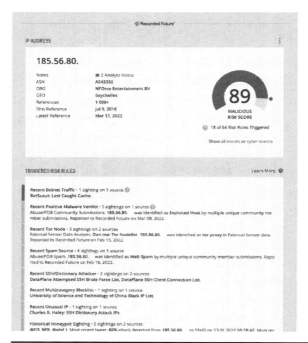

Figure 4-5: A SecOps intelligence solution automatically enriches alerts with context such as previous sightings, associations with attack types and threat actors, and risk scores. (Source: Recorded Future)

This enrichment enables SecOps analysts to quickly identify the most significant threats and take immediate, informed actions to resolve them.

Enrichment empowers even relatively junior SecOps analysts to "punch above their weight" by making connections that otherwise would have required more experience than they have. It also provides a form of accelerated on-the-job training by supplying in-depth information about the latest threats.

TECH TALK

As an example of this upskilling for relatively junior analysts, suppose an alert is generated when an unknown external IP address attempts to connect over TCP port 445. Experienced analysts might know that a recent exploit for SMB has been used by ransomware to propagate itself and would identify the IP as likely to be compromised based on the owner, location, and open source data. An inexperienced analyst might not be able to make these connections unaided, but contextualized SecOps intelligence would show the analyst that other devices on the network use SMB on port 445 to transfer files and data between servers. It would also inform the analyst that the new exploit and ransomware have been associated with that IP address.

Shortening the "Time to No"

As important as it is for SecOps analysts to gather information about real threats more quickly and accurately, there is an argument to be made that the ability to rapidly rule out false alarms is even more important.

SecOps intelligence provides staff with the context required to triage alerts promptly and with far less effort. It prevents analysts from wasting hours pursuing alerts based on:

- ☑ Actions that are likely to be innocuous rather than malicious
- ☑ Attacks that are not relevant to their organization
- ☑ Attacks for which defenses and controls are already in place

Some SecOps intelligence solutions automatically perform much of this filtering by customizing risk feeds to ignore or downgrade alerts that do not match organization- and industry-specific criteria.

Security Teams See a 40% Reduction in Investigation Time

A Forrester Consulting Total Economic Impact™ study, commissioned by Recorded Future, has found that users of Recorded Future intelligence realize benefits which include greater security operations efficiency, increased ability to avoid security breaches, and better defense of their brand value. To read the full study report, go to https://go.recordedfuture.com/forrester-tei-study.

Chapter 5

SecOps Intelligence Part 2 – Response

In this chapter

- Learn how intelligence minimizes reactivity
- Review characteristics of SecOps intelligence solutions that make them effective for meeting incident response challenges
- Explore incident response teams' use cases for intelligence

After real attacks have been identified, incident response processes kick in. But both of these workflows have become more stressful for security teams. Among the reasons:

☑ Cyber incident volumes have increased steadily for two decades.

☑ Threats have become more complex and harder to analyze; staying on top of the shifting threat landscape has become a major task in itself.

☑ When responding to security incidents, analysts are forced to spend significant time manually checking and disseminating data from disparate sources.

☑ Containment of attacks and eradication of vulnerabilities continually grow more difficult.

As a result, incident response teams routinely operate under enormous time pressures and often are unable to contain cyber incidents promptly.

Continuing Challenges

While it's difficult to be precise about the number of incidents experienced by a typical organization, there is no doubt that cyberattack volume is growing. While some of this growing pressure is mitigated by preventative technologies, a huge additional strain is nonetheless being placed on incident response teams because of the following factors.

A skills gap

Incident response is not an entry-level security function. It encompasses a vast swath of skills, including static and dynamic malware analysis, reverse engineering, and digital forensics. It requires analysts who have experience in the industry and are able to perform complex operations under pressure.

The highly publicized cybersecurity skills gap has grown consistently wider over the past decade. Cyber Seek calculates that there are almost 600,000 cybersecurity job openings in the United States alone. According to the ISSA-ESG report "The Life and Times of Cybersecurity Professionals 2021," 57 percent of organizations are negatively impacted by the shortage of cybersecurity professionals.

Rising response times

When you have too few skilled personnel and too many alerts, there's only one outcome: The time to resolve genuine security incidents will increase. According to the "2021 Cost of a Data Breach Report" from Ponemon Institute and IBM Security, the time to detect and contain a data breach increased from 257 days in 2017 to 287 days in 2021.

Of course, cybercriminals have no such constraints. Once they gain a foothold inside a target network, the time to compromise is usually measured in minutes. We will discuss this more in the next chapter.

A piecemeal approach

Most organizations have security groups that grow organically in parallel with increases in cyber risk. As a result, many only add security technologies and processes to address specific needs, and they do so without a strategic design.

While this ad hoc approach is perfectly normal, it forces incident response teams to spend a lot of time aggregating data and context from a variety of security technologies (e.g., SIEM, EDR, and firewall logs) and threat feeds. This effort significantly extends response times and increases the likelihood of mistakes.

The Reactivity Problem

Once an alert is flagged, it must be triaged, remediated, and followed up on as quickly as possible to minimize cyber risk. Consider a typical incident response process:

1. **Incident detection** — Receive an alert from a SIEM, EDR, or similar product.

2. **Discovery** — Determine what has happened and how to respond.

3. **Triage and containment** — Take immediate actions to mitigate the threat and minimize damage.

4. **Remediation** — Repair damage and remove infections.

5. **Push to BAU** — Pass the incident to "business as usual" teams for final actions.

Notice the reactive nature of this process. For most organizations, nearly all the work necessary to remediate an incident is back-loaded, meaning it can't be completed until after an alert is flagged. Although this is inevitable to some degree, it is far from ideal when incident response teams are already struggling to resolve incidents quickly enough.

Minimizing Reactivity in Incident Response

To reduce response times, incident response teams must become less reactive. Two areas where advanced preparation is especially impactful are identification of probable threats and prioritization.

Identification of probable threats

When an incident response team identifies the most commonly faced threats in advance, it enables them to develop strong, consistent processes to cope with them. This preparation dramatically reduces the time the team needs to contain individual incidents and prevent mistakes, and it frees up analysts to address new and unexpected threats when they arise.

Prioritization

Not all threats are equal. When incident response teams understand which threat vectors pose the greatest level of risk to their organization, they are able to allocate their time and resources accordingly.

Strengthening Incident Response With Intelligence

It should be clear from our discussion so far that security technologies *alone* can't do enough to reduce pressure on human analysts.

SecOps intelligence reduces the demands on incident response teams and addresses many of the issues we have been reviewing by:

- ☑ Automatically identifying and dismissing false positive alerts
- ☑ Enriching alerts with real-time context from across the open web, the dark web, and technical sources
- ☑ Assembling and comparing information from internal and external data sources to identify genuine threats
- ☑ Scoring and prioritizing threats according to the organization's specific needs and infrastructure

In other words, intelligence — especially SecOps intelligence — provides incident response teams with exactly the actionable insights they need to make faster, better decisions, while holding back the tide of irrelevant and unreliable alerts that typically make their job so difficult.

SecOps Intelligence in Action

Let's look at three use cases and one abuse case that show how SecOps intelligence affects incident response teams in the real world.

Use case: Prepare processes in advance

As noted earlier, typical incident response processes are highly reactive, with most activity happening only after an incident occurs. This extends the time needed to scope and remediate incidents.

SecOps intelligence enables incident response teams to prepare for threats by providing:

- ☑ A comprehensive, up-to-date picture of the threat landscape
- ☑ Information about popular threat actor TTPs
- ☑ Highlights of industry- and region-specific attack trends

SecOps intelligence empowers incident response teams to develop and maintain strong processes for the most common incidents and threats. Having these processes available speeds up incident discovery, triage, and containment. It also greatly improves the consistency and reliability of actions across the incident response function.

Use case: Scope and contain incidents

When an incident occurs, incident response analysts must make quick determinations about three factors:

1. What happened
2. What the incident might mean for the organization
3. Which actions to take

These factors must be analyzed as quickly as possible with a high degree of accuracy. SecOps intelligence makes a measurable impact by:

- ☑ Automatically dismissing false positives, enabling teams to focus on genuine security incidents
- ☑ Enriching incidents with related information from across the open and dark web, making it easier to determine how much of a threat they pose and how the organization might be affected
- ☑ Providing details about the threat and insights about the attacker TTPs, empowering the team to make fast and effective containment and remediation decisions

Use case: Remediate data exposure and stolen assets

It's common for organizations to take a long time to realize a breach has occurred. According to the IBM "Cost of a Data Breach Report 2021," the average time to identify a data breach is 212 days.

Not surprisingly, stolen data and proprietary assets often turn up for sale on the dark web before their rightful owners realize what's happened.

A powerful SecOps intelligence capability provides a tremendous advantage by alerting you to a breach and providing early warning that your assets are exposed online, or someone is offering those assets for sale.

Obtaining this intelligence in real time is vital because it enables you to contain the incident as quickly as possible and identify when and how your network was breached.

Abuse case: Half measures are worse than nothing

We want to caution you about one abuse case where intelligence may actually undermine incident response.

At the start of their intelligence journey, some organizations opt for a minimalist solution such as a SecOps intelligence solution paired with a variety of free threat feeds. They might believe that this "dip our toes in the water" approach will minimize up-front costs.

While this type of implementation arms incident response teams with some actionable intelligence, it generally makes things worse by forcing analysts to wade through vast quantities of false positives and irrelevant alerts. To fully address the primary incident response pain points, a SecOps intelligence capability must be comprehensive, relevant, contextualized, and integrated.

Essential Characteristics of SecOps Intelligence for Incident Response

Now it's time to examine the characteristics of a powerful SecOps intelligence capability, and how they address the greatest pain points for incident response teams.

Comprehensive

To be valuable to incident response teams, intelligence must be captured automatically from the widest possible range of locations across open sources, technical feeds, and the dark web. Otherwise analysts will be forced to conduct their own manual research to ensure nothing important has been missed.

TECH TALK

Imagine that an analyst needs to know whether an IP address has been associated with malicious activity. If she is confident that her intelligence has been drawn from a comprehensive range of threat sources, she is able to query the data instantly and be sure the result will be accurate. If she isn't confident, she will have to spend time manually checking the IP address against several threat data sources. Figure 5-1 shows how SecOps intelligence might connect an IP address with the Trickbot malware. This kind of intelligence can be correlated with internal network logs to reveal indicators of compromise.

Figure 5-1: Intelligence connecting an IP address with the Trickbot malware. (Source: Recorded Future)

ON THE WEB

For a discussion of how to distill massive quantities of data to produce a small but steady stream of actionable intelligence, read the Recorded Future blog post, "Optimize Your Security Tech Stack With SecOps Intelligence" (https://www.recorded-future.com/secops-intelligence-module-overview/).

Relevant

It's impossible to avoid all false positives when working to identify and contain incidents. But SecOps intelligence empowers incident response teams to quickly identify and purge false positives generated by security technologies such as SIEM and EDR products.

There are two categories of false positives to consider:

1. Alerts that are relevant to an organization but are inaccurate or unhelpful

2. Alerts that are accurate and/or interesting but *aren't* relevant to the organization

Both types have the potential to waste an enormous amount of an incident response analyst's time.

Advanced SecOps intelligence products are now employing powerful algorithms and analytical processes to identify and discard false positives automatically and draw analysts' attention to the most important (i.e., most relevant) intelligence.

CAUTION If you don't choose your SecOps intelligence technology carefully, your team is likely to waste a great deal of time on intelligence that's inaccurate, outdated, or irrelevant to your organization.

Contextualized

Not all threats are created equal. Even among relevant threat alerts, some will inevitably be more urgent and important than the rest. An alert from a single source could be both accurate and relevant, but still not particularly high in priority. That is why context is so important: It provides critical clues about which alerts will most likely matter to your organization.

Contextual intelligence related to an alert might include:

- ☑ Corroboration from multiple sources that the same type of alert has been associated with recent attacks
- ☑ Confirmation that it has been associated with threat actors known to be active in your industry
- ☑ A timeline showing that the alert occurred slightly before or after other events linked with attacks

Modern analytics and algorithms make it possible for a SecOps intelligence solution to consider multiple sources concurrently and determine which alerts are most important to a specific organization.

Integrated

Among the most critical characteristics of a SecOps intelligence product is its ability to integrate with a broad range of security tools, including SIEM and incident response solutions. Through integration, the product is able to examine the alerts they generate and:

☑ Determine whether each alert should be dismissed as a false positive

☑ Score the alert according to its importance

☑ Enrich the alert with valuable, real-time context and evidence

Effective integration eliminates the need for analysts to manually compare each alert to information found across their ecosystem of security and intelligence tools. Even more important, integration and automated processes are able to filter out a huge number of false positives *without any oversight by a human analyst.* Saving time and avoiding frustration are perhaps SecOps intelligence's greatest benefits for incident response teams.

Chapter 6

Vulnerability Intelligence

In this chapter

- Examine the current challenges to addressing vulnerabilities
- Learn how vulnerability intelligence delivers insights into threat actor behaviors
- See how risk-based intelligence streamlines the operational elements of vulnerability management

Vulnerability management is not glamorous, but it is one of the very few ways to be proactive in securing your organization. Its importance cannot be overstated.

The key to success in vulnerability management is to shift the thinking of your security teams from trying to patch everything to making risk-based decisions. That is critical because the vast ocean of vulnerabilities disclosed each year puts incredible stress on the teams responsible for identifying vulnerable assets and deploying patches. To make smart risk-based decisions, take advantage of more sources of intelligence.

The Vulnerability Problem by the Numbers

According to the Gartner Market Guide for Security Threat Intelligence Products and Services, about 8,000 vulnerabilities a year were disclosed over the past decade. The number increased only slightly from year to year, and only about one in eight of those vulnerabilities were actually exploited. However, during the same period, the amount of new software coming into use grew immensely, and the number of threats has increased exponentially.

In other words, although the number of breaches and threats has increased over the past 10 years, only a small percentage were based on new vulnerabilities. As Gartner puts it, "More threats are leveraging the same small set of vulnerabilities."

Zero day does not mean top priority

Zero-day threats regularly draw an outsized amount of attention. However, the vast majority of new threats labeled as zero days are actually variations on a theme, exploiting the same old vulnerabilities in slightly different ways. The implication is that the most effective approach to vulnerability management is not to focus on zero-day threats, but rather to identify and patch the vulnerabilities in the software your organization uses.

Time is of the essence

Threat actors have gotten quicker at exploiting vulnerabilities. According to Gartner, the average time it takes between the identification of a vulnerability and the appearance of an exploit in the wild has dropped from 45 days to 15 days over the last decade.

This trend has two implications for vulnerability management teams:

1. You have roughly two weeks to patch or remediate your systems against a new exploit.

2. If you can't patch in that timeframe, you need a plan to mitigate the damage.

Research from IBM X-Force shows that if a vulnerability is not exploited within two weeks to three months after it is announced, it is statistically unlikely that it ever will be exploited. Therefore "old" vulnerabilities are usually not a priority for patching.

ON THE WEB For insights on recent vulnerabilities, read the Recorded Future threat analysis "2021 Vulnerability Landscape" (https://www.recordedfuture.com/2021-vulnerability-landscape/).

DON'T FORGET All of these statistics point to one conclusion: Your goal should not be to patch the most vulnerabilities, or even the most zero-day threats, but rather to identify and address the vulnerabilities most likely to be exploited against your organization.

Assess Risk Based on Exploitability

Consider this comparison: If patching vulnerabilities to keep your network safe is like getting vaccines to protect yourself from disease, then you need to identify which vaccinations are priorities and which are unnecessary. You may need a flu shot every season to stay healthy, but there's no need to stay vaccinated against yellow fever or malaria unless you will be exposed to them.

Two of the greatest values of a vulnerability intelligence solution are identification of specific vulnerabilities that represent actual risk to your organization and visibility into their likelihood of exploitation.

Figure 6-1 illustrates the point. Thousands of vulnerabilities have been disclosed. Hundreds are being exploited, and some number of vulnerabilities exist in your environment. You really only need to be concerned about the ones that lie within the intersection of those last two categories — vulnerabilities that are in your environment and are actively being exploited.

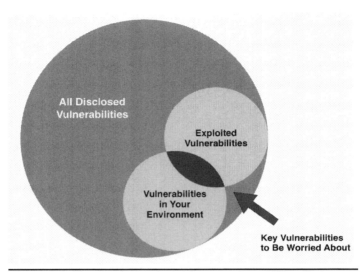

Figure 6-1: The greatest actual risks are vulnerabilities that are present in your organization's environment and are currently being exploited. (Source: Gartner)

CVSS scores are often misleading

Ranking threats in terms of severity is a mistake that vulnerability managers make regularly. Classification and ranking systems like Common Vulnerabilities and Exposures (CVE) naming and Common Vulnerability Scoring Systems (CVSSs) don't take into account whether threat actors are actually exploiting vulnerabilities right now in your industry or locations. It's important to keep in mind that threat actors don't care about CVSS scores.

The Genesis of Intelligence for Security Teams: Vulnerability Databases

Vulnerability databases consolidate information on disclosed vulnerabilities and also score their exploitability.

In fact, one of the very first forms of intelligence for security teams was NIST's National Vulnerability Database (NVD). It centralizes information on disclosed vulnerabilities to make it easier for organizations to see if they were likely to be affected. For more than 20 years, the NVD has collected information on more than 150,000 vulnerabilities, making it an invaluable source for information security professionals. Nations including China and Russia have followed NIST's lead by setting up vulnerability databases.

ON THE WEB Find the NIST NVD at https://nvd.nist.gov/. A catalog of vulnerability databases is published by the industry organization FIRST here: https://www.first.org/global/sigs/vrdx/vdb-catalog.

CAUTION There are two significant limitations to most vulnerability databases:

1. They focus on technical exploitability rather than active exploitation.

2. They are not updated fast enough to provide warning of some quickly spreading threats.

Exploitability versus exploitation

Information in vulnerability databases is almost entirely focused on technical exploitability – a judgment of how likely it is that exploiting a particular vulnerability will result in greater or lesser damage to systems and networks. In the NVD, this is measured through the CVSS scoring system.

Technical exploitability and active exploitation are not the same thing, though. CVSS base scores provide a metric that's reasonably accurate and easy to understand, but you need to know what information the score is conveying. Unless a base score is modified by a temporal score or an environmental score, it really only tells you how bad the vulnerability is hypothetically, not whether it's actually being exploited in the wild.

Figure 6-2 shows the kind of valuable information that a vulnerability intelligence tool provides. In this case, the risk a vulnerability poses is determined based on reports involving the CVE's appearance before it has been assigned a CVSS score by NVD.

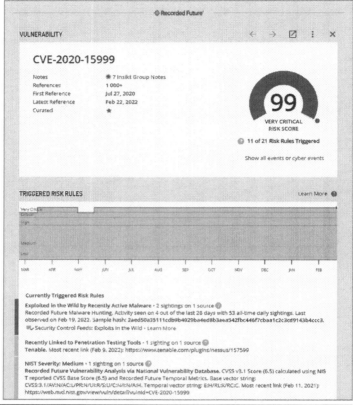

Figure 6-2: Intelligence related to a vulnerability. (Source: Recorded Future)

TECH TALK

An object lesson in the difference between the NVD's "official risk" and "real risk" from a vulnerability in the wild is CVE-2020-15999. Despite having a CVSS severity score of only 6.5 (in the medium range), Recorded Future considered it a very high risk due to recent evidence of widespread exploitation.

Next week versus now

Lack of timeliness is another shortcoming of many vulnerability databases. For example, an analysis by Recorded Future found that 75 percent of disclosed vulnerabilities appear on other online sources before they appear in the NVD — and on average it takes those vulnerabilities a week to show up there. This is a very serious problem, because it handicaps security teams in the race to patch a vulnerability before adversaries are able to exploit it, as illustrated in Figure 6-3.

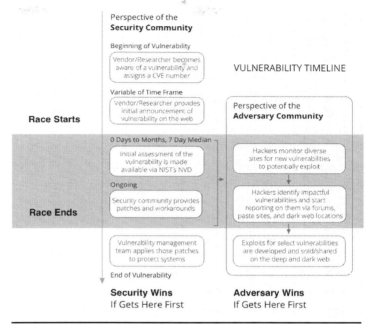

Figure 6-3: The race between security professionals and adversaries. (Source: Recorded Future)

TECH TALK

The informal way in which vulnerabilities are disclosed and announced contributes to the delay in recognizing them in vulnerability databases. Typically, a vendor or researcher discloses the vulnerability to the NVD, which assigns a CVE number and begins an analysis. In the meantime, the vendor or researcher publishes more information on its own blog or a social media account. Good luck collating data from these disparate and hard-to-find sources before threat actors develop proof-of-concept malware and add it to exploit kits!

ON THE WEB

For details on the processes that threat actors use to exploit vulnerabilities, see the Recorded Future blog post "Behind the Scenes of the Adversary Exploit Process" (https://www. recordedfuture.com/adversary-exploit-process/).

Vulnerability Intelligence and Real Risk

The most effective way to assess the true risk of a vulnerability to your organization is to combine all of the following:

- ☑ Internal vulnerability scanning data
- ☑ External intelligence from a wide variety of sources
- ☑ Business context such as asset criticality and network exposure
- ☑ An understanding of why threat actors are targeting certain vulnerabilities and ignoring others

Internal vulnerability scanning

Almost every vulnerability management team scans internal systems for vulnerabilities, correlates the results with information reported in vulnerability databases, and uses the correlation to determine what to patch. This is a basic use of operational intelligence, even if we don't usually think of it that way.

Conventional scanning is an excellent way to *deprioritize* vulnerabilities that don't appear on your systems. By itself, however, scanning is not an adequate way to accurately prioritize vulnerabilities that are found.

Risk milestones for vulnerabilities

One powerful way to assess a vulnerability's risk is to look at how far it has progressed from initial identification to availability, weaponization, and commoditization in exploit kits.

The level of real risk increases dramatically as the vulnerability passes through the milestones shown in Figure 6-4. Broad-based vulnerability intelligence reveals a vulnerability's progress along this path.

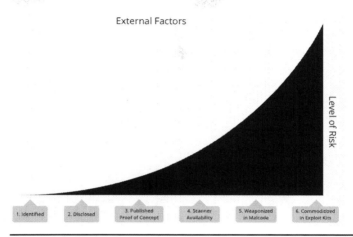

External Factors

1. Identified | 2. Disclosed | 3. Published Proof of Concept | 4. Scanner Availability | 5. Weaponized in Malcode | 6. Commoditized in Exploit Kits

Level of Risk

Figure 6-4: Real risk rises dramatically when vulnerabilities become weaponized and commoditized. (Source: Recorded Future)

Understanding the adversary

As discussed elsewhere in this book, good intelligence should not simply provide information in the form of scores and statistics. That's why vulnerability intelligence leads to a deeper understanding of how and why threat actors are targeting certain vulnerabilities and ignoring others. Below we discuss sources of intelligence that contribute to this understanding.

How to Create Meaningful Risk Scores

Beyond technical characteristics, what are the factors that can be used to calculate risk scores of vulnerabilities? Recorded Future's native risk scoring system incorporates data about criminal adoption, patterns in exploit sharing, and the number of links to malware. This information often comes from sources that are difficult to access, like forums on the dark web.

Sources of Intelligence

Data from asset scans and external vulnerability databases are only the starting points for generating intelligence that enables you to assess the risk of vulnerabilities. Unless vulnerability intelligence includes data from a wide range and variety of sources, analysts risk missing emerging vulnerabilities until it's too late.

Valuable sources of information for assessing true risk to your business include:

- ☑ **Information security sites** like vendor blogs, official disclosure information on vulnerabilities, and security news sites
- ☑ **Social media,** where link sharing provides jumping-off points for uncovering useful intelligence
- ☑ **Code repositories** such as GitHub, which yield insights into the development of proof-of-concept code for exploiting vulnerabilities
- ☑ **Paste sites** such as Pastebin and Ghostbin (which are sometimes wrongly defined as dark web sources) that often house lists of exploitable vulnerabilities
- ☑ **The dark web**, composed of communities and marketplaces with a barrier to entry, where exploits are developed, shared, and sold
- ☑ **Forums** with no barrier to entry or requirement to be using specific software, where threat actors exchange information on vulnerabilities and exploits
- ☑ **Technical feeds** that deliver data streams of potentially malicious indicators, which add useful context around the activities of malware and exploit kits

Vulnerability Chatter on the Dark Web

There are several reasons why it's difficult (and potentially dangerous) to eavesdrop on the channels that threat actors use to communicate and operate:

- Underground forums are hard to find (after all, there's no Google for the dark web).

- Threat actors change locations whenever they feel their anonymity is at risk.

- It takes a lot of searching to find the crumbs of information that are relevant to your security.

- Access may require entrance fees or endorsements from existing members of the community.

- Many of these forums operate exclusively in local languages.

Intelligence vendors with expertise in collecting and analyzing dark web intelligence come into play here. They offer contextualized information from dark web forums on vulnerabilities directly relevant to your network, without putting you or your organization in harm's way.

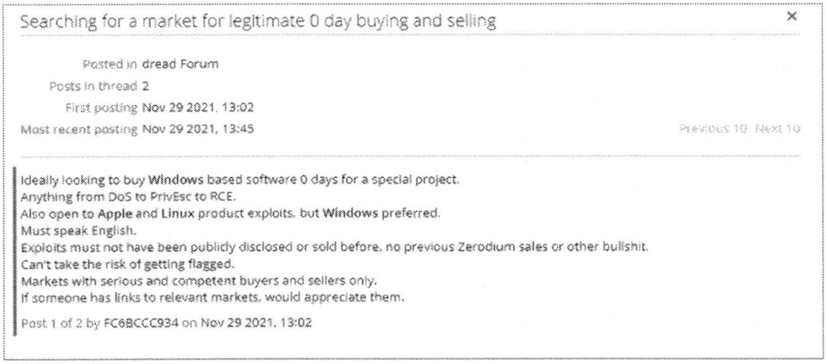

Searching for a market for legitimate 0 day buying and selling　　×

Posted in dread Forum
Posts in thread 2
First posting Nov 29 2021, 13:02
Most recent posting Nov 29 2021, 13:45　　　　　Previous 10　Next 10

Ideally looking to buy **Windows** based software 0 days for a special project.
Anything from DoS to PrivEsc to RCE.
Also open to **Apple** and **Linux** product exploits, but **Windows** preferred.
Must speak English.
Exploits must not have been publicly disclosed or sold before, no previous Zerodium sales or other bullshit.
Can't take the risk of getting flagged.
Markets with serious and competent buyers and sellers only.
If someone has links to relevant markets, would appreciate them.

Post 1 of 2 by FC6BCCC934 on Nov 29 2021, 13:02

Figure 6-5: An exchange of information between threat actors on a dark web forum translated from Russian. (Source: Recorded Future)

Use Cases for Cross-Referencing Intelligence

To accurately assess real risk, you must be able to correlate information from multiple sources. Once you begin to understand how individual references combine to tell the whole story, you will be able to map the intelligence you have to the risk milestones a vulnerability typically goes through.

For example, you might notice a new vulnerability disclosed on a vendor's website. Then, you discover a tweet with a link to proof-of-concept exploit code on GitHub. Later, you find the code is being sold on a dark web forum. Eventually, you might see news reports of the vulnerability being exploited in the wild.

Here's another example. The website of an Information Sharing and Analysis Center (ISAC) for your industry shows that an organization like yours has been victimized by an exploit kit that attacks a vulnerability in a specialized, industry-specific software application. You find that there are four copies of that software in corners of your organization that have not been patched in three years.

 TIP Cross-referencing this kind of intelligence enables you to move away from a "race to patch everything" mode of operation, and empowers you to focus on the vulnerabilities that present the greatest actual risk.

Bridging the Risk Gaps Among Security, Operations, and Business Leadership

In most organizations, the responsibility for protecting against vulnerabilities falls on the shoulders of two teams:

1. The vulnerability management team runs scans and prioritizes vulnerabilities based on potential risk.

2. The IT operations team deploys patches and remediates the affected systems.

This dynamic creates a tendency to approach vulnerability management "by the numbers." For example, the vulnerability management team in the security organization might determine that several vulnerabilities in Apache web servers pose a very high risk to the business and should be given top priority. However, the IT operations team may be supporting a lot more Windows systems than Apache servers. If team members are measured strictly on the number of systems patched, they have an incentive to keep their focus on lower-priority Windows vulnerabilities.

Intelligence on exploitability also prepares your organization to strike the correct balance between patching vulnerable systems and interrupting business operations. Most organizations have a strong aversion to disturbing business continuity. However, if you know that a patch will protect the organization against a real, imminent risk, then a short interruption is completely justified.

The risk milestones framework outlined in Figure 6-4 makes it much easier to communicate the danger of a vulnerability across your security and operations teams, up through senior managers, and even to the board of directors. This level of visibility into the rationale behind decisions made around vulnerabilities will increase confidence in the security team across your entire organization.

 TIP To reduce the gap between the vulnerability management and IT operations teams, introduce risk of exploitability as a key driver for prioritizing patches. Arming the vulnerability management team with more contextualized data about the risk of exploitability will enable them to pinpoint a smaller number of high-risk CVEs, which will result in them making fewer demands on the operations team. The operations team will then be able to give top priority to that small number of critical patches, and still have time to address their other goals.

Chapter 7

Threat Intelligence
Part 1 – Knowing Attackers

- Explore the role of threat analysts
- See how conversations in underground communities present opportunities to gather valuable intelligence
- Examine use cases for applying knowledge about attackers to security activities

Our Definition of "Threat Intelligence"

Until recently, many of the topics discussed in this handbook were known throughout the security community as "threat intelligence." However, the term threat intelligence has become closely associated with information about direct threats to traditional IT systems. We now use "intelligence for security teams," or just "intelligence" to include that information, plus additional details about risks related to areas such as third parties, brand presence on websites and social media platforms outside of the corporate network, risks to physical assets around the globe, and more.

This shift has not eliminated the need for threat intelligence. It is still essential to enable threat analysts to perform their most important functions, including:

☑ Identifying the actors who most actively threaten the organization

☑ Understanding attackers' motives and targets

☑ Investigating and documenting their TTPs

☑ Tracking macro trends that affect the organization, including trends relevant to its industry and the regions where it operates

An intelligence solution is essential to the success of threat analysts, because it pinpoints the most relevant threats, slashes the time they spend researching them, and generates more intelligence about them — often from sources that would be difficult or impossible for analysts to find and access on their own.

In this chapter and the next we will examine several of the main responsibilities of threat analysts.

Understand Your Enemy

Threat analysts cannot focus solely on detecting and responding to threats already present in their environment. They need to anticipate attacks by gathering intelligence about the cybercriminal gangs, state-sponsored hacking groups, ideological "hacktivists," and others who target their organizations.

As an example, let's look at the kind of intelligence you might be able to find about profit-motivated cybercriminal gangs. They are an important intelligence target, because the "Verizon 2021 Data Breach Investigations Report" (https://www.verizon.com/business/resources/reports/dbir/2021/) attributes 80 percent of confirmed breaches to organized crime (Figure 7-1).

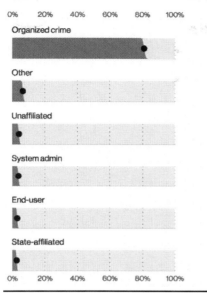

Figure 7-1: Top external actor varieties in data breaches. (Source: Verizon Data Breach Investigation Report 2021)

Intelligence gathered by Recorded Future from global dark web communities shows that organized criminal groups (OCGs) are employing freelance workers to defraud businesses and individuals. These groups operate just like legitimate businesses in many ways, with a hierarchy of members functioning as a team to create, operate, and maintain fraud schemes.

A typical OCG is controlled by a single mastermind (Figure 7-2). It might include specialists with relevant expertise for the crimes they commit. For example, bankers with extensive connections in the financial industry may arrange money laundering, forgers might be responsible for fake documents and supporting paperwork, professional project managers could oversee the technical aspects of operations, software engineers would write code, and other skilled coders may be involved for specific tasks. Some groups even include ex-law enforcement agents who gather information and run counter-intelligence operations.

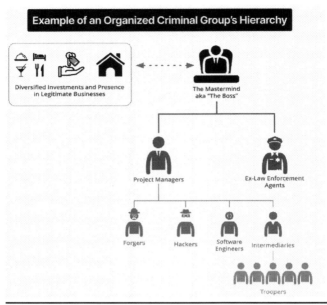

Figure 7-2: A typical organizational chart for a cybercrime syndicate. (Source: Recorded Future)

The members of cybercrime syndicates tend to have strong ties in real life, and often are respected members of their social groups. They certainly don't regard themselves as ordinary street criminals. They rarely cross paths with what most people think of as traditional gangsters, preferring to remain in the shadows and avoid attention from law enforcement and local mafia branches. However, schemes that require large numbers of people, such as those that involve taking cash out of multiple automated teller machines simultaneously, may involve a chain of intermediaries who recruit and manage the troopers who do the leg work.

Criminal Communities and the Dark Web

Only rarely are threat analysts able to attribute a cyberattack to a single individual operating in isolation. Advanced attacks typically require a wide range of skills and tools, and an infrastructure capable of launching and supporting campaigns that use ransomware, phishing, and other technical tools and social engineering techniques.

Today, all those products and services are available for purchase or for rent in a sophisticated underground criminal economy. Cybercriminals and their accomplices exchange information and carry out transactions related to illicit activities on the deep web (areas of the web that are not indexed by search engines) and the dark web (areas of the web that are only accessible with special software and tools that mask the identity of visitors).

Gated communities

Not all threat actors operate exclusively in what would technically be referred to as the dark web. Some build communities based on fairly standard discussion boards that are encrypted behind a login and use web collaboration technologies like Jabber and Telegram to conduct their business.

Prospective members of these underground networks are vetted by active participants in the chat rooms and forums before they are allowed to join. They may have to pay an entrance fee, ranging from US$50 to $2,000 or more. In fact, at least one forum is known to require a deposit of more than $100,000 from prospective members.

A strength — and a weakness

The dark web and criminal communities give threat actors access to information, tools, infrastructure, and contract services that multiply their power and reach. However, these communities also create risks for threat actors, because they are susceptible to monitoring — which provides intelligence that enables security teams to anticipate and defeat attacks.

Know Your Dark Networks

We found that the dark web is organized in three distinct communities: low-tier underground forums, higher-tier dark web forums, and dark web markets. Analysis revealed that a significant group of actors are posting in both low-tier and higher tier forums, showing a connection between these two communities. However, dark web markets are largely disconnected from these forums. Gain a deeper understanding of how the criminal underground maintains a hierarchy of users by reading this research from Recorded Future: "Dark Networks: Social Network Analysis of Dark Web Communities."

Connecting the Dots

Intelligence gathered from underground communities is a window into the motivations, methods, and tactics of threat actors, especially when this intelligence is correlated with information from the surface web, including technical feeds and indicators.

The power of truly contextualized intelligence is demonstrated by its ability to draw together data from a wide variety of sources and make connections between disparate pieces of information.

For example, the following contextual information might be used to turn news about a new malware variant into intelligence:

- ☑ Evidence that threat actors are using this malware in the wild
- ☑ Reports that exploit kits using the malware are available for sale on the dark web
- ☑ Confirmation that vulnerabilities targeted by the exploit kits are present in your organization

TIP

Monitor the dark web and underground communities for direct mentions of your organization and assets. These mentions often indicate targeting or potential breaches. It's also important to monitor for mentions of your industry and other less specific terms that might point to your operations. Using threat intelligence to assess risk in this way will give you greater confidence about your defenses and empower you to make better decisions.

Use Case: More Comprehensive Incident Response

When indicators of a threat are detected, SecOps teams take immediate steps to protect the targeted assets. However, they rely on threat analysts to research the attack and provide additional information to more fully shut down the attack, remediate its effects, and prevent future occurrences.

For example, threat analysts are often able to attribute an attack to a particular cybercriminal or state-sponsored hacking group and research the group's TTPs. Security teams might then use that intelligence to take steps like finding other instances of malware and phishing emails used in the attack, cleaning up affected systems, quarantining the emails, forcing password changes for compromised accounts, and taking other steps to disrupt the attacker's kill chain.

DON'T FORGET

Research for thorough incident response and remediation takes a significant amount of time. To achieve rapid response, it is critical to use an intelligence solution with automation and integration to collect and process large volumes of data from many sources and find relevant context and insights. The intelligence solution must also be able to automate workflows for analyzing the intelligence and disseminating it quickly to the right security teams and management, within their existing security tools and in their preferred formats.

Use Case: Proactive Threat Hunting

Most security programs are reactive, meaning they rely on alerts before taking action. However, many organizations are creating threat hunting teams to look proactively for indicators of threats before an alert is generated and ideally before the attack has progressed very far.

There are hundreds of clues that threat hunters may search for on networks and endpoints. These include: Malware files, suspicious changes to registry keys, system configurations and application permissions, unusual DLLs, scripts and drivers, misuse of utilities like PowerShell and PSExec, anomalous behaviors by JOB files, binaries that initiate connections outside of the corporate network, unusual sequences of events (such as applications that download and execute scripts on start-up), and techniques used to steal credentials.

Intelligence solutions provide detailed profiles of the threat actors currently attacking similar organizations and the techniques and tools they use. This information enables threat hunters to avoid "boiling the ocean" by trying to capture and analyze vast amounts of data. Instead, they are able to prioritize searches for the most dangerous threats to their organization and focus on finding specific indicators and artifacts related to those attacks.

To strengthen threat hunting, explore the use of Network Traffic Analysis (NTA). NTA involves monitoring and analyzing network data to identify anomalies and provide insight and context on malicious infrastructure connected to your network. Attackers use these malicious connections to send commands, receive information updates, and exfiltrate data. Through NTA, an organization can detect malicious hosts connecting to a network and warn when those connections exfiltrate data. NTA provides real-time, actionable intelligence that warns security teams about adversary actions and shows how far their attacks have progressed.

Use Case: Advance Warning of Payment Fraud

Since the birth of commerce, criminals have looked for ways to use available technology to make an easy profit from those in possession of assets. In 17th century England, for example, the growth in coach travel among an affluent merchant class, combined with the invention of the portable flintlock pistol, gave rise to the highwayman.

In our digital age, companies that conduct business and transact online find their data targeted by various forms of cyber fraud, including payment fraud.

The term "payment fraud" encompasses a wide variety of techniques by which cybercriminals profit from compromised payment data. For example, they may use phishing to collect payment card details. More-complex attacks might compromise ecommerce sites or point-of-sale systems to achieve the same goal. Once they have acquired card data, the criminals resell it (often as packs of numbers) and walk away with their cut.

One example of the effective use of threat intelligence is providing threat analysts with advance warning of upcoming attacks related to payment fraud. Monitoring sources like underground communities, paste sites, and other forums for relevant payment card numbers, bank identifier numbers, or references specific to financial institutions potentially provides visibility into nefarious operations that might affect their organization. Then the analysts can work with other security teams to forestall the planned attacks by remediating relevant vulnerabilities, increasing monitoring of targeted systems, and tightening security controls. Chapter 12 has more information on using intelligence to thwart payment fraud.

Chapter 8

Threat Intelligence Part 2 – Risk Analysis

- Explore the value of risk models like the FAIR framework
- Discover right and wrong ways to gather data about risk
- Learn how intelligence enables you to forecast attack probabilities and the financial costs of attacks

A key function of threat analysts is to model risks and empower managers to make informed decisions about reducing risk. Risk modeling offers a way to objectively assess current risks, and to estimate clear and quantifiable financial returns from investments in cybersecurity.

However, many cyber risk models suffer from either:

☑ Vague, non-quantified output, often in the form of "stoplight charts" that show green, yellow, and red threat levels

☑ Estimates about threat probabilities and costs that are hastily compiled, based on partial information, and riddled with unfounded assumptions

Non-quantified output is not very actionable, while models based on faulty input result in "garbage in, garbage out" scenarios with outputs that appear to be precise, but are actually misleading. To avoid these problems, organizations need a well-designed risk model and plenty of valid, current information — including threat intelligence.

Cybersecurity risk assessments should not be based only on criteria defined to prove compliance with regulations. With those criteria, assessing risk usually becomes an exercise in checking boxes against cybersecurity controls like firewalls and encryption. Counting the number of boxes checked results in a very misleading picture of actual risk.

The FAIR Risk Model

The equation at the core of any risk model is simple:

"Likelihood of occurrence times impact equals expected cost."

But, clearly, the devil is in the details. Fortunately, some very smart people have developed effective risk models and methodologies that you can use and adapt to your own needs. One that we like is the Factor Analysis of Information Risk (FAIR) model from the FAIR Institute. Figure 8-1 shows the framework of this model.

The FAIR framework is useful for creating a quantitative risk assessment model that contains specific probabilities for loss from specific kinds of threats.

Learn more about FAIR at the FAIR Institute website. This quantitative model for information security and operational risk is focused on understanding, analyzing, and quantifying information risk in real financial terms.

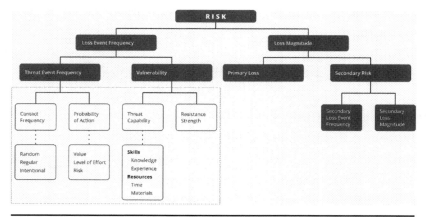

Figure 8-1: The FAIR Framework, with elements informed by intelligence highlighted. (Source: The FAIR Institute)

Measurements and transparency are key

The FAIR framework (and others like it) enable you to create risk models that:

- ☑ Make defined measurements of risk

- ☑ Are transparent about assumptions, variables, and outcomes

- ☑ Show specific loss probabilities in financial terms

Measurements, formulas, assumptions, variables, and outcomes need to be made transparent in order to be discussed, defended, and changed. Because much of the FAIR model is defined in business and financial terms, executives, line of business managers, and other stakeholders can learn to speak the same language to classify assets, threats, and vulnerabilities in the same way.

TIP Whenever possible, incorporate specific probabilities about future losses in your risk model. Specific probabilities enable risk managers and senior executives to discuss the model and potential ways to improve it, after which their confidence in the model and the recommendations that come out of it will increase.

Which Statement Is More Useful?

"The threat from DDoS attacks to our business has been changed from high to medium (red to yellow)."

Or

"There is a 20 percent probability that our business will incur a loss of more than $300,000 in the next 12 months because a distributed denial-of-service (DDoS) attack will disrupt the availability of our customer-facing websites."

Intelligence and Threat Probabilities

As shown in the left side of Figure 8-1, a major part of creating a threat model involves estimating the probability of successful attacks (or "loss event frequency" in the language of the FAIR framework).

The first step is to create a list of threat categories that might affect the business. This list typically includes malware, phishing attacks, exploit kits, zero-day attacks, web application exploits, DDoS attacks, ransomware, and many other threats.

The next step is much more difficult: To estimate probabilities that the attacks will happen, and that they will succeed (i.e., the odds that the organization contains vulnerabilities related to the attacks and existing controls are not sufficient to stop them).

CAUTION

Avoid the following scenario: A GRC (governance, risk, and compliance) team member asks a security analyst, "What is the likelihood of us facing this particular attack?" The security analyst (who really can't win) thinks for 30 seconds about past experience and current security controls and makes a wild guess: "I dunno, maybe 20 percent."

To avoid appearing clueless, your security team needs answers that are better informed than that. Intelligence makes it possible to answer questions such as:

- ☑ Which threat actors are using this attack, and do they target our industry?
- ☑ How often has this specific attack been observed recently by organizations like ours?
- ☑ Is the trend up or down?
- ☑ Which vulnerabilities does this attack exploit, and are those vulnerabilities present in our organization?
- ☑ What kind of damage, technical and financial, has this attack caused in organizations like ours?

Threat analysts still need to know a great deal about the organization and its security defenses, but threat intelligence enriches their knowledge of attacks, the actors behind them, and their targets. It also provides hard data on the prevalence of the attacks.

Figures 8-2 and 8-3 show some of the forms the intelligence might take. Figure 8-2 lists the kinds of questions about a malware sample that an intelligence solution answers for analysts.

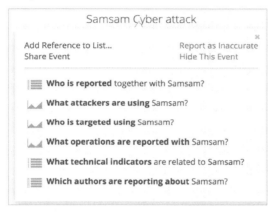

Figure 8-2: Questions about a malware sample that an intelligence solution answers. (Source: Recorded Future)

Figure 8-3 shows trends in the proliferation of ransomware families. The trend line to the right of each ransomware family indicates increasing or decreasing references across a huge range of threat data sources such as code repositories, paste sites, security research blogs, underground forums, and .onion (Tor accessible) forums. Additional information might be available about how the ransomware families connect to threat actors, targets, and exploit kits.

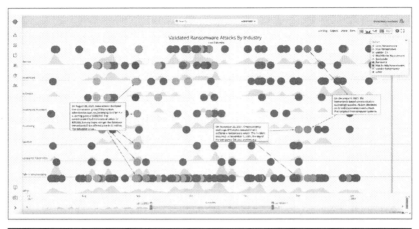

Figure 8-3: Timeline depicting the proliferation of new ransomware families. (Source: Recorded Future)

Intelligence and the Financial Cost of Attacks

The other major component of the formulas in our model is the probable cost of successful attacks. Most of the data for estimating cost is likely to come from inside the organization. However, threat intelligence provides useful reference points on topics like:

- ☑ The cost of similar attacks on organizations of the same size and in the same industry
- ☑ The systems that need to be remediated after an attack, and the type of remediation they require

We will discuss risk management more in Chapter 15, including the Threat Category Risk (TCR) framework which was developed by Levi Gundert of Recorded Future, and is explained in detail in his book, "The Risk Business, What CISOs Need to Know About Risk-Based Cybersecurity" (https://go.recordedfuture.com/the-risk-business).

Chapter 9

Third-Party Intelligence

In this chapter

- Explore the impact of increasing third-party risk and understand why static assessment of that risk falls short
- Learn about top risks you should monitor
- See why using real-time, automated intelligence is the best way to mitigate third-party risk

Third-Party Risk Looms Large

Because businesses and their supply chains are so tightly integrated, it's critical to consider the security of your partners, vendors, and other third parties when assessing the risk profile of your own organization.

A recent survey by the Ponemon Institute, "Digital Transformation & Cyber Risk: What You Need to Know to Stay Safe," found that 55 percent of organizations have had a breach that originated from a third party, and only 29 percent believe their partners would notify them of a compromise. Related statistics are shown in Figure 9-1.

Third-Party Risk Is Real

 55%
of organizations have experienced a data breach originated from a third party

 58%
of organizations do not have a third-party cyber risk management program

 53%
of organizations say their tools for managing third-party risk are only somewhat effective or are not effective

Figure 9-1: Most organizations are exposed to significant risks through their relationships with third parties. (Source: Ponemon Institute)

The writing is on the wall: Third-party attacks will continue to increase and get worse, they will further complicate cyber risk management, and your partners probably won't tell you about their most critical problems.

Traditional third-party risk assessment methods rely on static outputs, like self-assessments, financial audits, monthly reports about new vulnerabilities discovered in the systems an organization uses, and occasional reports on the status of security control compliance. However, static assessments become outdated quickly, because they fail to reflect the dynamic nature of a changing business. In short, you don't have the information they need to make informed decisions about managing third-party risks to your organization.

In contrast, real-time intelligence about third parties enables you to accurately assess risk posed by those organizations and keep assessments current as conditions change and new threats emerge.

Traditional Risk Assessments Fall Short

Many of the most common third-party risk management practices employed today lag behind security requirements. Static assessments of risk — like financial audits and security certificate verifications — are still important, but they often lack context and timeliness.

Organizations following traditional approaches to managing third-party risk often use these three steps:

1. They attempt to understand their organization's business relationship with a third party and how it exposes their organization to threats.

2. Based on that understanding, they identify frameworks to evaluate the third party's financial health, corporate controls, and IT security and hygiene, as well as how these factors relate to their own organization's approach to security.

3. Using those frameworks, they assess the third party to determine whether it is compliant with security standards like SOC 2 or FISMA. Sometimes they conduct a financial audit of the third party.

While these steps are essential for evaluating third-party risk, they don't tell the whole story. The outputs are static and cannot reflect quickly changing conditions and emerging threats. The analysis is often too simplistic to produce actionable recommendations. Sometimes, the final report is opaque, making it impossible to dig deeper into the methodology behind the analysis. All of these factors create blind spots that leave decision-makers unsure whether crucial pieces of information might have been overlooked.

When assessing third-party risk, do not rely entirely on self-reporting questionnaires or a vendor's inwardly focused view of their own security defenses. Round these out with an external, unbiased perspective on the vendor's threat landscape.

A Thought Experiment

Imagine that you went through the traditional steps of a risk assessment, as outlined above. You concluded that one vendor in your supply chain is safe to work with.

Now, this supplier experiences a ransomware attack that may or may not have exposed your organization's internal data. How long would it take your vendor to disclose the attack? Are you able to accurately determine what, if any, proactive security measures you need to take and how quickly you need to act?

What to Look for in Third-Party Intelligence

To accurately evaluate third-party risk in real time, you need a solution that offers immediate context on the current threat landscape. Third-party intelligence provides critical risk indicators that enable you to determine which shortcomings in your supply chain partners' defenses represent meaningful risks to your organization. Those include not only the current risks present at the time of assessment, but also a historical view — which provides even more insight to detect, prevent, and resolve risks.

To effectively evaluate third-party risk, a third-party intelligence solution needs to offer:

1. Access to a diverse range of risk data from the open web, dark web, and technical sources

2. Automation and analytics to quickly and comprehensively sort massive data into an easily consumable risk score with actionable recommendations

3. Transparent evidence for faster risk analysis and risk mitigation

4. Real-time alerts on changes and newly emerging risks

5. Ongoing visibility into your partners' ever-changing environments

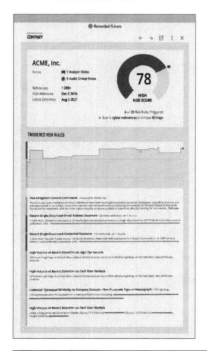

Figure 9-2: Third-party intelligence provides context for identifying shortcomings in the defenses of supply chain partners. (Source: Recorded Future)

Monitor Third Parties for These Five Critical Risks

Ransomware

Ransomware attacks have been growing dramatically in scope and impact. A few recent attacks have disrupted entire sectors of the U.S. economy. An attack on the Colonial Pipeline system in May 2021 created chaos for gas stations and motorists and significant problems for refineries, airlines, and other industries that produce and consume fuel. The same month, an attack on meat processor JBS sent large segments of the livestock and restaurant industries into disarray.

An example of even more egregious third-party risk on a global scale came to light in July 2021. The REvil cybercrime group infected the software of Kaseya, a company providing a solution to manage workstations and servers in remote locations. Most of the roughly 60 Kaseya customers compromised were managed service providers. Because each service provider was accessing the networks of many customers, REvil was able to launch ransomware attacks against more than 1,500 businesses around the world, and claimed to have encrypted files on more than one million systems.

Recently the cybercrime organizations behind many ransomware campaigns have added a new weapon to their toolbox: "double extortion ransomware." In double extortion ransomware attacks, before malware encrypts data on the victim's systems, it exfiltrates copies to servers controlled by the cybercriminals. The attackers then publish samples of the victim's sensitive information on a ransomware extortion website, together with ransom demands and payment instructions. The threat of exposing intellectual property or sensitive financial and customer data gives the cybercriminals even more leverage in ransom negotiations.

If one of your partners is hit by a double extortion ransomware attack, that is definitely bad news for them. However, there is a silver lining for you. If you monitor ransomware extortion websites, you will get early notice that the partner has been compromised. When this happens, you can:

☑ Assess the nature of your relationship with the organization and determine what sort of response is necessary

☑ Notify your partner so they can determine which systems have been impacted and isolate them

☑ Change credentials or cut off VPN access to ensure the attacker can't access your systems

☑ Identify the type of malware used against the third party and ensure that your defenses can counter it

☑ Switch to an alternative source to ensure business continuity in case your partner's operations are affected

Speed of response is critical. If you can take action while the negotiations between the attacker and the victim are still going on, you may be able to harden your defenses before the attackers turn their attention to you.

Data breaches

What if your third-party partners are slow to tell you about security incidents? What if it takes weeks or months before they realize they have been breached?

You don't have to remain in the dark. Websites on the open web and dark web can provide evidence that your partners have been compromised. This evidence includes design documents and other intellectual property, personally identifiable information about customers and employees, proprietary software code, and credentials and technical information about the partners' information systems. The information can turn up in dark web marketplaces and on hacker forums, paste sites, and code repositories.

Also, many breaches are disclosed on news sites on the open web and in social media. Of course, you may need extensive language expertise to take advantage of these resources.

If you find any of these indicators that a partner has been compromised, you can:

☑ Inform your partner so they contain the attack and determine the root causes

☑ Work with the partner to discover if any of your data was lost in the breach

☑ Reevaluate the terms of your relationship with the partner, and if necessary require them to upgrade their security controls and processes

Malicious network activity

Cyberthreat models such as the Lockheed Martin Cyber Kill Chain® illustrate that advanced cyberattacks involve a lot of network communication between systems controlled by the attacker and the target organizations. Threat actors use servers and bots to send phishing emails that contain malware or links to counterfeit websites that capture credentials. Malware and scripts planted in the target's network create command and control (C&C) channels to exchange information about the victim's environment and instructions on how to find and collect sensitive data. As a final step, captured data is exfiltrated to the attacker's servers.

Many of the servers and bots used by adversaries are "known bad." That is, during investigations of previous attacks their IP addresses have been associated with malicious or suspicious activities. These IP addresses have been collected and published by cybersecurity vendors, industry consortiums, and government agencies, and many enterprises block web traffic between them and their own environment.

But what about monitoring the network traffic of your suppliers, contractors, service providers, and others who have access to your systems? Malicious network activity provides insight into planned and ongoing attacks on third parties. If you find such indicators you can:

☑ Log the malicious IP addresses and share them with your partner, so they can block traffic to the malicious websites

☑ Work with the partner to determine if they have already been compromised and to improve their controls to stop spam, malware, and C&C traffic

☑ Change the partner's credentials for your systems

☑ Check that you have blocked traffic from your own networks to the malicious websites and that your defenses can counter the attacks being used against the partner

Exposed credentials

You give partners credentials so they can integrate their operations with yours. But credentials are literally "the keys to the kingdom." Threat actors who obtain credentials to one of your partner's information systems have the power to steal your information residing there, shut down the partner's operations, and impersonate the partner to access your systems. Because credentials are so valuable, many attackers make a special effort to find and exfiltrate them during data breaches.

Which brings us to another example of dark clouds with a silver lining.

Cybercriminals have created a niche economy to buy and sell credentials. Some hackers specialize in acquiring credentials through phishing attacks, keyloggers and other malware, social engineering, and password spraying (brute force testing of common passwords). Some data breaches aimed primarily at intellectual property or personal information sweep up credentials at the same time. In both cases attackers may use dark web marketplaces to sell the stolen credentials to other cybercriminals who specialize in advanced attacks. The sellers often provide information about the specific organizations that issued the credentials.

These dark web marketplaces make cybercriminality more efficient. However, you can monitor dark web forums and marketplaces, as well as paste sites, dump sites and other places where stolen credentials are exposed. If you find credentials providing access to one of your partners, you can:

☑ Offer your findings to the partner so they can disable the accounts with the stolen credentials

☑ Change the partner's credentials for your systems

☑ Help the partner analyze how the credentials were stolen and how similar thefts can be prevented

☑ Work with the partner to determine if the stolen credentials are being used in an ongoing attack, and if necessary help them contain the attack

Plotting on the dark web

On the dark web, cybercriminals and hackers communicate and transact business anonymously (and in fairness to the dark web, so do journalists and dissidents living under repressive governments). Users of the dark web typically hide behind nicknames ("handles") to conceal their identities and use TOR browsers and networks to obfuscate their IP addresses. Many forums and marketplaces on the dark web implement the digital equivalent of a nightclub rope line with a bouncer: would-be members are turned away unless they have been invited or can pass a test.

Threat actors often use forums on the dark web to plan attacks and to recruit other cybercriminals—and sometimes corrupt company insiders—to assist them. Politically motivated actors and "hacktivists" sometimes use the same forums to justify their actions or boast of their prowess. The participants in these forums frequently name their targets.

If you monitor dark web forums, you can uncover plotting against your partners (as well as your enterprise). Observing activity in these forums provides early warning of attacks and information about the tactics, techniques, and procedures that will be used.

With this information you can:

☑ Warn your partners so they can configure or upgrade their defenses to thwart the tactics and techniques of the attackers

☑ Ensure that your defenses are able to protect against the same attacks

☑ Notify law enforcement organizations so they can take down or impede the threat actors

Responding to High Third-Party Risk Scores

What do you do when faced with high risk scores for a third party? Not every data breach justifies terminating business with that partner. Just about every organization contends with cyberattacks and unexpected downtime, and partners are no exception. The more important issue is how they (and you) deal with incidents and take steps to reduce future risks.

A change in risk scores may present an opportunity to talk with your business partners about their approach to security. On your end, it's important to look more closely at whether the risk rules that were triggered will impact your organization's network. For example, a partner's risk score might increase because typosquatting websites closely resembling legitimate websites operated by the partner were discovered. Putting those sites on the deny list in your own network is one way to thwart phishing campaigns while you investigate what steps that partner plans to take to protect its brand identity.

For smart security decisions that involve your third parties, you need up-to-the-minute context and evidence provided by third-party intelligence.

Chapter 10

Brand Intelligence

In this chapter

- Review the many forms of digital risk to brands
- Learn how intelligence identifies and remediates attacks against brands online

---

Brand protection involves safeguarding an organization's image, reputation, and customers from attacks that primarily never touch its network or systems. Most organizations lack visibility into these types of attacks. Threats include:

- ☑ Fake websites and social media accounts used to impersonate the organization or its employees for fraud and phishing attacks
- ☑ Malicious content and false information about the organization and its products posted on websites and social media platforms
- ☑ Counterfeit products and software offered in digital marketplaces and app stores
- ☑ Data leaks and leaked credentials from employees and executives

Most of these threats are posed by financially motivated criminals, but they may also involve hacktivists, dissatisfied customers, competitors, and careless or disgruntled employees who reveal information online.

Protect your brand and your customers

To truly protect your brand, you need to be concerned about threats that leverage it to harm or influence your customers. Customers who are lured into a scam or fraud from an imitation of your website may hold your organization responsible. Those who buy a low-quality, counterfeit version of your product from an online marketplace may lose trust in your brand. Those who think one of your executives has published offensive content on the web may boycott your products — even if it wasn't your executive who posted it. Pleading "it wasn't our fault" won't restore their trust or your reputation in any of these scenarios.

A Different Kind of Detection

Most of the activities we have been discussing in this handbook involve creating intelligence about attackers and their tools. Brand intelligence includes some of that, as well, but the emphasis is instead on detecting your organization's name and brand everywhere they occur across the internet.

You need to be rigorous about listing and searching for mentions of all your brand and product names, and keywords that are associated with them. These include the names of:

- ☑ Your parent organization

- ☑ Subsidiaries and business units

- ☑ Products

- ☑ Executives

- ☑ Managers and employees who engage with the public in web forums and via social media

It also includes logos, trademarks, service marks, and advertising slogans that appear on your organization's authorized websites, since these are frequently used on phony websites.

Uncovering Evidence of Brand Impersonation and Abuse

Knowing what to look for empowers you to find evidence of brand impersonation and abuse in places many organizations never search. For example, a brand intelligence solution enables you to:

☑ Search domain registries to find domain names that include your organization or product name, or variations of them

☑ Crawl the web to find typosquatting domains

☑ Monitor social media to alert you to hashtags that include your organization or product name, or variations of them

☑ Scan social media to detect accounts that claim to belong to your organization, your executives, or your employees

☑ Check app stores to uncover unauthorized mobile apps using your branding

☑ Comb web forums for threat actors planning to impersonate your brand

Use case: Typosquatting and fraudulent domains

Typosquatting involves manipulating the characters in an organization's domain name into nearly identical domains. For instance, threat actors targeting example.com might create a typosquat URL of exanple.com. Attackers often register thousands of domains differing by a single character from their target organizations' URLs. They do this for reasons ranging from suspicious to fully malicious.

Rogue websites using these modified domain names are built to look like legitimate websites. The rogue domains and websites are often used in spear-phishing campaigns against employees or customers, watering-hole attacks, and drive-by download attacks.

Being alerted to newly registered phishing and typosquatting domains in real time is the best way to narrow the window of opportunity for threat actors to impersonate your brand and defraud unsuspecting users. Once the malicious infrastructure is identified, you're able to employ a takedown service to nullify the threat.

Uncovering Evidence of Breaches on the Web

By monitoring the web — including private forums on the dark web — brand intelligence solutions enable you to uncover evidence of data breaches within your organization and partner ecosystem. You may find:

☑ Your customers' names and data

☑ Financial account data and Social Security numbers

☑ Leaked or stolen credentials from your employees

☑ Paste and bin sites containing your proprietary software code

☑ Forums mentioning your organization and announcing intentions to attack it

☑ Forums selling tools and discussing techniques to attack organizations like yours

Timely discovery of these indicators enables you to:

☑ Secure the sources of the data

☑ Find and fix vulnerabilities and misconfigurations in your infrastructure

☑ Mitigate future risks by improving security controls

☑ Identify ways to improve employee training and coding practices

☑ Enable your SecOps and incident response teams to recognize attacks faster

TIP It's often possible to narrow down the source of a leak by looking at exactly what information and artifacts are found on the web, where they are found, and what else is found in the same place. For example, if you find product designs or software code on a dark web site and recognize that they were shared with only a few suppliers, you would know to investigate the security controls of those suppliers as part of your third-party risk management program. If your organization's name was mentioned on an underground forum whose members are known to attack certain applications, you could increase protection of the targeted applications by patching the systems they run on, monitoring them more closely, and adding security controls.

Use case: Compromised data

Threat actors make money from many types of compromised personal information and corporate intellectual property. Examples of compromised data for sale on the dark web include medical records, cloned and compromised gift cards, and stolen credentials to "pay for" services like music streaming providers or transportation applications, and items charged via online payment providers, as illustrated in Figure 10-1.

Time	Event Information
	Credential leak targeting @hotmail.com
	⚡x200 FRESH ACCOUNTS ⚡
MAR 8 2022	@hotmail.com:@30*5/1994 <https://www. .com/password>" Forum Thread
	Source Cracked Forum by ILostmyDowen on Mar 8, 2022, 17:43
	Resolved https://www. .com/password to www. .com
	https://CrackedTo%20Forums%20(Obfuscated)/Thread-Streaming-%E2%9A%A1%EF%B8%8Fx200-FRESH-ACCOUNTS%E2%9A%A1%EF%B8%8F?pid=18241669#pid18241669 · Reference Actions · 4+ references

Figure 10-1: Compromised data – Credentials for an online music-streaming service disclosed on the dark web. (Source: Recorded Future)

A high percentage of hacking-related breaches leverage stolen or weak passwords. Threat actors regularly upload massive caches of usernames and passwords to paste sites and the dark web, or make them available for sale on underground marketplaces. These data dumps may include corporate email addresses and passwords, as well as login details for other sites.

Monitoring external sources for this type of intelligence will dramatically increase your visibility — not just into leaked credentials, but also into potential breaches of corporate data and proprietary code.

Disinformation Is Alarmingly Simple and Inexpensive

Spreading lies about an organization on the web is easy and cheap. As a learning exercise, Recorded Future's Insikt Group* used a disinformation service provider to launch a negative campaign against a fictional corporation for just $4,200.

The exercise

Insikt Group created a fictitious company. It then found two disinformation service providers on Russian-speaking underground forums and commissioned them to generate intentionally false narratives across the web. One was asked to create positive propaganda to make the company seem appealing. The other was tasked with spreading malicious material accusing the same company of unethical business practices.

The results

Insikt Group discovered that launching disinformation campaigns is alarmingly simple and inexpensive. Both misinformation campaigns produced results in less than a month for only a few thousand dollars: $1,850 for the positive propaganda effort and $4,200 for the negative disinformation campaign. The service providers disseminated their messages successfully by placing articles on reputable web sites and creating social media accounts of seemingly real people.

The conclusions

- Disinformation services are publicly available on underground forums.

- For a few thousand dollars, disinformation service providers will publish articles in media sources ranging from dubious websites to reputable news outlets.

- These service providers use a combination of established and new social media accounts to propagate content without triggering content moderation controls.

Learn about the methods used by disinformation service providers in Insikt Group's cyber threat analysis report: "The Price of Influence: Disinformation in the Private Sector" (https://go.recordedfuture.com/hubfs/reports/cta-2019-0930.pdf).

Critical Qualities for Brand Intelligence Solutions

Of course, mitigating digital risk to your brand is not simply a matter of stumbling across one typosquatting domain or some isolated piece of stolen data. Somebody, or something, has to do the broader work of collecting masses of data, sifting through thousands of data points, analyzing relationships among the data points, deciding priorities, and ultimately taking action.

The best approach is to use a brand intelligence solution that:

- ☑ **Collects and scans data from the broadest range and variety of sources**: Automation at the data-collection stage saves analysts precious time. The best solutions gather data not only from open web sources, but also from the dark web and technical sources.

- ☑ **Maps, monitors, and scores brand risk**: Through automation, advanced data science, and analytical techniques like natural language processing, effective brand intelligence tools enable analysts to link business attributes with related digital assets and detect, score, and prioritize events related to brand risk.

- ☑ **Coordinates remediation**: Robust brand intelligence solutions generate alerts and reports that provide information on how to remediate problems. Alerts automatically update security or marketing teams as new information arises. The solutions also offer services to take down various types of brand attacks.

Case Study: Defeating Typosquatting at a Large HR Solutions Provider

A large human resources, health, and wealth benefits services provider enables other organizations to manage their human resources. This company handles a lot of personally identifiable information (PII) — including sensitive health and financial data. To protect that data, they have an extensive security operations center, featuring 24/7/365 monitoring, incident response, investigation and forensics, and more.

Their vice president of security operations says that at one time it took a team of around 100 people to manage these functions. With Recorded Future, it takes 10. "Obtaining a list of all the mentions of our company across the internet by the end of the day was totally infeasible, even if I had 10 or 20 people working on it," the VP says.

The VP adds, "Sure, we could spend a lot of money to get people burner accounts and access to these private spaces, but what a waste! Anything beyond two people makes no sense compared to just using Recorded Future. The cost is less than two headcount, versus the 10 or 20 I would need to try to do something similar."

For example, one morning an alert went off about a potential typosquatting domain. The alert was triggered by a monitoring rule the team had set up in Recorded Future to check for fraudulent domains that resemble ones owned by the organization. Registering these domains is often the first step in a phishing attack.

As soon as the team got the alert, they investigated and found phishing attempts targeting their organization and some of their clients. They immediately sent out a flash report to their whole organization and all their clients and partners. The report provided actionable recommendations on how to counter the attack: Block the domain at your proxy and use event logs to scan for the threat with your SIEM. Many of their partners reported hits from the site, but they were able to block access before any damage was done.

Thanks to real-time brand intelligence, the company was able to mitigate the threat in a matter of hours, rather than weeks — or never.

Chapter 11

Geopolitical Intelligence

- Understand the factors that cause geopolitical risk
- Discover all the groups that use geopolitical intelligence
- Explore geofencing and geopolitical risk event types

What Is Geopolitical Risk?

Geopolitical risk is exposure to risk from shifting strategic and tactical global trends in every geographic region that could impact your organization.

Think about a country or city where your organization has an office or a facility such as a factory, an office, a warehouse, or perhaps a clinic, consulate, or military base. The operations of that facility could be affected by:

☑ Decisions and actions by government bodies and agencies — from passing legislation, to introducing regulations, to mobilizing police or military forces in a state of emergency

☑ Actions by political parties, trade unions, activist groups, and other organizations — including strikes, demonstrations, protests, boycotts, social media campaigns, and even riots and targeted attacks on physical locations and property

☑ Natural and man-made disasters — such as disease outbreaks, hurricanes and earthquakes, military actions, and terrorist attacks

The effects of these events range from temporary disruptions, to millions of dollars in direct and indirect costs, to loss of life.

High Impact

A recent survey of global organizations with revenue of $250 million or more found that more than 90% of executives worldwide believe that their company has been affected by unexpected political risks in the past 12 months. Changes in trade and industrial policies are affecting operating decisions in areas such as diversifying the supplier base, modifying merger and acquisition strategies, adjusting the length of supply chains, and moving toward nearshoring and onshoring. (Source: EY-Parthenon: "Geostrategy in Practice 2021")

The authors of an earlier version of the study (Geostrategy in Practice 2020) highlighted four types of political risk:

- Risks arising from conflicts between countries and changes in international systems

- Risks related to national political environments, the stability of governments and institutions, and legislation

- Risks that emerge when governments change environmental, health and safety, financial market, and other regulations

- Risks created by activism on the part of groups such as trade unions and consumer bodies

Geopolitical Intelligence

Consider the advantages of being warned days before these types of events impact your organization, or being alerted in real time when they occur. That knowledge may enable you to prevent the events from affecting your organization — or it might put you in a position to respond faster when mitigating their effect.

Additionally, intelligence about local attitudes and long-term trends provides the insights you need to make smarter determinations about expanding operations into specific countries and cities.

Location, location, location

Geopolitical intelligence uses the intelligence life cycle described in Chapter 3. The main difference between geopolitical intelligence and other types of intelligence for security teams is the starting point.

Intelligence activities for security operations, incident response, vulnerability management, threat analysis, and third-party risk teams are organized primarily around threats and threat actors. Brand intelligence focuses on names and keywords related to the organization's brands and products.

In contrast, geopolitical intelligence starts with geographical locations and geopolitical trends — typically in the cities, countries, and regions where your organization has physical assets and facilities. Its output is facts and insights about location-specific events that have a potential impact on the operations of those facilities and the staff there.

Supply chains, customers, and geopolitical risk

Geopolitical risk is not just about your organization's offices and facilities. As illustrated in 2020 and 2021, during the COVID-19 pandemic, disruptions that affect supply chain partners and transportation networks also have a dramatic effect on the operations of an organization. This is true even in regions where the organization has no physical assets or personnel. When location-specific events affect a large number of its customers or clients, an organization may struggle as a result.

Who Uses Geopolitical Intelligence?

Geopolitical intelligence is valuable to many groups within organizations that are global or aspire to expand globally. The names of the groups often differ across various organizations, but may include the following teams:

- ☑ Physical security

- ☑ Security operations

- ☑ Global security

- ☑ Business continuity

- ☑ Supply chain management

- ☑ Risk management

☑ Government relations

☑ Strategic intelligence

☑ Public policy or public affairs

☑ Office of the general counsel

☑ Regional and national management

These groups have a variety of responsibilities related to geopolitical risks, including:

☑ Anticipating and preventing harm (e.g., closing a facility before a mass demonstration)

☑ Responding quickly to mitigate the effects of events (e.g., providing aid to employees or finding alternate sources of supply after a natural disaster)

☑ Communicating key facts to employees, customers, business partners, and government agencies

☑ Assessing location-based risks in the future to guide investment and expansion decisions

DON'T FORGET

To get the most out of geopolitical intelligence, consult with these groups about their information needs, and use that input to set priorities for intelligence collection and analysis. Tailor your output to be easily understood and actionable by these audiences. See the "Direction" and "Dissemination" sections of the intelligence life cycle discussion in Chapter 3.

Data Collection With Geofencing

To empower your organization to anticipate and cope with location-specific events, you need to start by selecting the locations and types of events that matter to your organization. The geopolitical intelligence solution will then monitor and filter data by location, which is called "geofencing."

TIP

If your organization has a physical security, global security, or business continuity department, that team likely maintains a list of all of your office and facility locations around the world.

DON'T FORGET Dig even deeper than your list of offices and facilities by asking different groups in your organization about supply chain partners, transportation networks, clients and customers, and other entities that may affect your operations. Document the locations where they might be susceptible to geopolitical events, and monitor them.

You also need to specify the event types to monitor. Figure 11-1 is an example of high-level geopolitical event categories and some of the specific items that might be offered within one category.

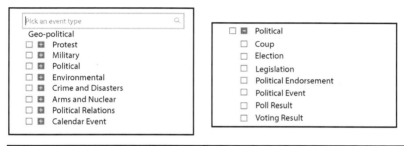

Figure 11-1: Examples of geopolitical event categories and the specific items within one category. (Source: Recorded Future)

Data and Information Sources

The sources of data and information used to produce geopolitical intelligence overlap with those used for other types of intelligence. Technical sources such as threat feeds typically play a smaller role in geopolitical intelligence, because most cyber threats are not location-specific. The most valuable geopolitical intelligence sources tend to be specific to a country or city, for example:

- ☑ Global news and public media websites

- ☑ Social media posts

- ☑ Blogs

- ☑ Forums and marketplaces on both the open and dark web

Most of these sources include data and information from national and local governments, regulatory agencies, media organizations, trade unions, consumer groups, and individuals. However, activists and criminals also use the dark web to plan dangerous and illegal activities targeting specific locations — making dark web sources valuable for geopolitical intelligence.

Automation, Analytics, and Expertise

It takes an enormous amount of work to determine which sites, and which specific articles, videos, messages, and posts are relevant to a particular location and threat type. That's why organizations that are serious about managing geopolitical risk must use an intelligence platform that combines analytics, automation, and human expertise to process and analyze data and information.

Automation reduces, and often eliminates, resource-intensive, time-consuming manual research. It also speeds up processes for calculating and updating risk scores, disseminating alerts, creating visual representations of data, and many additional tasks.

Analytics are what enable an intelligence solution to collect millions of pieces of information from open web, dark web, and technical sources, and dynamically link and categorize them to generate intelligence about specified locations and geopolitical event types. Thanks to analytics, analysts don't need to manually comb through massive volumes of content, discover patterns, and connect the dots between facts and insights related to specific locations and threat types.

Specialized analytic tools assist in other areas as well. While most communication among threat actors is conducted in either English or Russian, government announcements, news stories, and social media and blog posts are naturally written in a variety of local languages. Natural language processing (NLP) is an analytic tool that identifies pieces of content that contain key words and phrases in every language. For example, NLP enables an intelligence solution to find relevant news articles, blog posts, and dark web chatter related to a message in a Russian-language forum that mentions "В Киеве будет протестный марш" (a protest march in Kyiv).

Of course, geopolitical intelligence is not just about automation and analytics. Often, there is no substitute for human expertise. This is particularly true when addressing issues related to specific regions and countries, where language skills (including knowledge of local slang) and familiarity with history and politics are critical. That is why you should also evaluate intelligence solutions on their ability to deliver finished intelligence — especially finished geopolitical intelligence.

Finished intelligence may include custom research reports evaluating risks in specific regions, tailored insights about the latest threats affecting those areas, and hunting packages that accelerate the research of your incident response, threat hunting, and geopolitical risk teams.

TECH TALK

For a technical discussion of how an intelligence platform combines analytics with human expertise and automation to categorize and connect huge volumes of security data, read the Recorded Future white paper, "The Security Intelligence Graph: Inside Recorded Future's Methodology and Patented Technology" (https://go.recordedfuture.com/security-intelligence-graph).

Interacting With Geopolitical Intelligence

Intelligence solutions enable you to access and interact with geopolitical intelligence in several formats, such as:

- ☑ Dashboards and maps showing risk levels by country and city

- ☑ Alerts triggered by events or changes in risk scores

- ☑ Reports detailing events and issues related to specified locations

- ☑ Background documents and insights summarizing key findings for countries and cities

- ☑ Integrations with other intelligence tools, for example the location intelligence provider Esri

In addition, some geopolitical intelligence solutions can integrate with more traditional security tools like SIEMs and ticketing systems and use geographical tags to ensure that people concerned with specific cities, countries, and regions receive immediate alerts of events there.

Figure 11-2 is an example of a geopolitical intelligence dashboard that highlights high-risk areas on a map of the world.

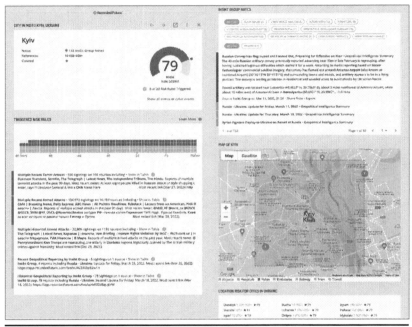

Figure 11-2: Example of a dashboard that highlights high-risk areas. (Source: Recorded Future)

Geopolitics and Cyber Threats

This chapter has focused on threats and events that originate in the same countries as the facilities you want to protect. However, geopolitical risk also involves, well, geopolitics: Political, economic, and ideological conflicts between nations and global alliances.

In the last several years the world has witnessed cyber attacks against internet, financial, and physical infrastructures.

Among these have been attempts to overload or disable the websites of government agencies, non-governmental organizations (NGOs), and independent media outlets; as well as misinformation campaigns targeting governments, elections, and businesses.

Most of these attacks have been attributed to mysterious hacking groups, sometimes linked to governments, and occasionally even to departments of a government or a military service. Many government agencies, commercial businesses, and NGOs are caught in the crossfire — even when they have little or no connection to the dispute between nations that started the conflict. This makes understanding the intersection between physical and cyber risk more important now than ever before.

Defending your organization against these types of threats requires a comprehensive intelligence program that encompasses all of the topics discussed in this handbook, from SecOps and threat intelligence to brand protection, and from vulnerability and third-party risk management to geopolitical intelligence.

ON THE WEB To learn more about the link between geopolitical conflicts and cyber threats, read the Recorded Future blog post, "Geopolitics: An Overlooked Influencer in Cyber Operations" (https://www.recordedfuture.com/geopolitical-cyber-operations/).To find out more about the connection between national rivalries and hacktivism, read, "Return to Normalcy: False Flags and the Decline of International Hacktivism" (https://www.recordedfuture.com/international-hacktivism-analysis/).

Chapter 12

Fraud Intelligence

In this chapter

- Review special challenges to preventing online fraud
- Learn how intelligence can be used to anticipate and thwart fraud campaigns

Fraud Intelligence and Risk Assessment

Fraud intelligence is concerned primarily with preventing credit card payment fraud, as well as other types of fraud related to online transactions. While fraud intelligence is most critical to financial institutions and retailers, it is also valuable for healthcare, government, travel, entertainment, online games, and other organizations that take payments online for goods and services.

Fraud intelligence differs in one important respect from most of the types of intelligence we have been discussing. When intelligence provides a list of vulnerabilities or misconfigurations that represent real threats to the enterprise, the goal is to eliminate them. However, when fraud intelligence points to a batch of payment card accounts that may have been compromised, banks, merchants, hospitals, and government agencies probably won't automatically block transactions or close accounts. Instead, they will take a risk-based approach to authorizing transactions (see text box). In these situations, fraud intelligence is used to help assess risk rather than create a list of vulnerabilities and issues that must be remediated.

Risk-Based Authorization

Today, most financial institutions and many ecommerce websites take a risk-based approach to authenticating users and authorizing transactions. For example, when a user requests a transaction, the application will assess its risk based on factors such as the value of the transaction, the user's device and its location, the user's behavior online and its similarities to previous behaviors, and known issues related to the user or the payment method. Depending on the risk calculation, the user may be asked to supply a password, answer security questions, or input a one-time code sent to a smartphone. Some transactions may be put on hold pending special approval or blocked entirely.

Fraud intelligence that improves the accuracy of risk assessments can have a major impact on reducing fraud.

Fraud intelligence involves collecting and correlating fragmentary data from many sources to identify exposed accounts and pinpoint the source of breaches. We will look now at specific ways it can be used to anticipate and thwart fraud campaigns.

Monitor Card Portfolio Exposure and Leaked Credentials

Like many other types of intelligence, fraud intelligence can be gathered from forums and marketplaces on the dark web. The type of evidence that can be found includes:

- ☑ Payment card bin numbers and other data often associated with payment card accounts such as names, street addresses, phone numbers, and zip codes

- ☑ Social Security numbers, driver's license numbers, dates of birth, frequent user numbers, and other data often associated with healthcare, government, travel, and other accounts

- ☑ Leaked credentials with employee email addresses and other identifiers

- ☑ "Chatter" about sites vulnerable to fraud and methods to bypass anti-fraud protections

- ☑ On rare occasions, actual payment card account numbers

Cybercriminals on the dark web rarely reveal payment card account numbers. Sometimes it is possible to acquire some account information by posing as a criminal buyer. However, usually this requires an established identity on the dark web and idiomatic language skills in Russian, Chinese, and other non-English tongues.

More often, it is necessary to collect fraud-related data from multiple sources and put pieces together to create actionable fraud intelligence. And since some of the information can be misleading or simply fake, it takes some work to clean up the data.

Still, the results can be very valuable to fraud protection and risk management groups. Frequently they can flag compromised accounts and adjust their organization's risk controls before fraud takes place.

Identify Compromised Common Points of Purchase

A key fraud protection technique is correlating many fraudulent transactions to identify compromised common points of purchase (CPPs). These are typically merchant websites (and sometimes physical locations) with a vulnerability that has been exploited to capture credit card numbers and user information for many accounts.

Identifying compromised CPPs provides several dividends:

- ☑ All customers who have visited the compromised CPP within the exposure period can be placed in a higher risk category to reduce or eliminate the chance that their accounts can be used for fraud
- ☑ The vulnerability on the site can be remediated to prevent future compromises
- ☑ The attacker's TTPs can be analyzed to improve the defenses of other websites

The more data on fraudulent transactions that is available, the easier it is to identify compromised CPPs. However, many financial institutions are reluctant to share this type of information with other enterprises in the same field. That is why industry organizations and fraud intelligence service providers often can collect more data and do a better job of finding compromised sites.

Monitor Websites for Magecart and Other Attacks

Another technique for acquiring fraud intelligence is to monitor merchant and other ecommerce websites for digital skimming attacks such as Magecart and iFrame injections. It is usually possible to identify websites that have been compromised by these attacks by inspecting site code in a browser, without requiring any actions by the merchant. This monitoring can reveal compromised data even before it has been offered for sale on the dark web or used to commit frauds.

Once compromised websites have been detected, it is often possible to:

- ☑ Identify numerous IOCs related to the attack
- ☑ Create a comprehensive picture of the attacker's infrastructure and methods, including phishing domains, exfiltration domains, and malicious code
- ☑ Reconstruct when accounts were exposed

This information can be used to find other websites victimized by the same attacker, protect other ecommerce websites, and identify accounts that may have been stolen and therefore should be placed in a high-risk category.

TECH TALK Magecart is a loose alliance of malicious hackers who started by targeting online shopping cart systems to inject card-skimming malware and capture payment card data. They have since branched out with additional techniques for deploying skimmers and capturing card data. Magecart attacks have grown in prominence since the beginning of the COVID-19 pandemic because they facilitate Card Not Present (CNP) fraud (fraud committed without the physical card, usually online).

ON THE WEB For more information on the evolution of Magecart attacks, see two Gemini Advisory blog posts: "Keeper" Magecart Group Infects 570 Sites (https://geminiadvisory.io/keeper-magecart-group-infects-570-sites/) and Gemini Annual Report 2021 (https://www.recordedfuture.com/gemini-annual-report-2021-magecart-thrives/). (Gemini Advisory is a Recorded Future company.)

Identify Signals

The dark web includes underground marketplaces where cybercriminals buy and sell software, services, and account information used for fraud campaigns. Monitoring these marketplaces can provide signals that attacks are imminent.

For example, criminals are willing to pay more for payment card account information when they know that fraud attempts are likely to be successful. A rise in the price of accounts for a payment card can signal that a weakness in fraud prevention controls for that card or for the bank that issued it have become known and that attacks are imminent. This intelligence alerts the issuing institution that it should increase its risk levels and review its security controls.

Fraudsters like to use credentials for cards in the location where the account holder lives because local use reduces the chance that a transaction will be flagged as suspicious. Therefore, a surge in dark web requests for accounts in a specific city or region can indicate that a criminal group is planning to launch attacks there. Financial institutions and merchants can respond by increasing risk controls for transactions in that area.

Outrunning the Other Guy

There is an old joke about two friends hiking in the woods who are surprised by an approaching bear. One friend immediately starts running away. The other opens his backpack and begins replacing his hiking boots with running shoes. "Are you crazy?" shouts the first friend, "You can't outrun a bear!" "I don't have to outrun the bear," says the second friend, "I only have to outrun you."

This logic applies to many fraud prevention scenarios. Even a slight improvement in the risk models of financial institutions and online merchants can yield outsized reductions in fraud rates.

Cybercriminal groups are diligent about tracking the return on investment of their campaigns. If they see an unusually low return on attacks against a specific payment card or merchant, they turn their attention to easier victims. Fraud intelligence can provide the edge that makes this happen.

Sometimes the effect of better fraud prevention can be observed in dark web marketplaces. When you see decreasing demand and falling prices for information on certain cards you are actually watching the bear turning to chase the other guy!

The ROI of Fraud Intelligence

Fraud intelligence typically yields a high return on investment for banks that issue payment cards. The proactive use of fraud intelligence:

☑ Prevents fraud

☑ Improves customer satisfaction and retention by reducing false-positive signals in purchase transactions

☑ Raises merchant retention and underlying revenues

Chapter 13

Identity Intelligence

In this chapter

- Examine the idea of collecting and analyzing compromised credentials to protect employees, partners, and customers
- Understand the need for wide coverage and high-volume triage
- Explore how to use intelligence to protect identities

Protecting Authentication

Strong identity authentication is essential for thwarting online fraud, account takeover (ATO) and ransomware attacks, thefts of PII and intellectual property, business email compromise (BEC) attacks, and other threats.

Cybercriminals have long recognized that user credentials are the proverbial keys to the castle. They have developed many innovative ways to obtain them, including skimming and key logging malware, phishing and social engineering attacks directed at end users, and data breaches of corporate, government, retail, and social media websites. People who reuse passwords on multiple accounts play into their hands, because credentials stolen in one data breach often can be used to penetrate many websites.

How serious is this issue? In the *2021 Trends in Securing Digital Identities* report from the Identity Defined Security Alliance and Dimensional Research, 95% of the companies surveyed acknowledged an identity-related breach at some point in time, and 79% said they had experienced an identity-related breach during the past two years. In its 2021 Data Breach Investigations Report, Verizon found that credentials were the most sought-after data type during breaches.

ON THE WEB The outlook for credential theft has gotten even worse with the emergence of stealer malware. A prime example is the RedLine Stealer malware sold on several dark web forums by a Russian-speaking cybercriminal who goes by the handle "REDGlade." RedLine Stealer captures usernames, passwords, cookies, payment card credentials and cryptocurrency wallet information from browsers, FTP clients, and instant messaging clients. It can be distributed through phishing emails, social media, and messaging applications, or embedded in a seemingly legitimate app. For a detailed overview, read RedLine Stealer is Key Source of Identity Data for Criminal Shops, a report published by the Insikt Group of Recorded Future (https://go.recordedfuture.com/hubfs/reports/mtp-2021-1014.pdf).

A Plan to Protect Identities

But all is not lost. Real-time intelligence about compromised credentials can disrupt adversaries before their attacks cause any damage. Imagine that you could compile a database of all the stolen identities published and sold on the dark web. You would be able to:

- ☑ Scan the user accounts of your employees, as well as contractors and business partners who have access to your systems, to identify and change credentials that have been compromised

- ☑ Perform automatic risk checks during critical events such as password creations and resets, to prevent people from reusing exposed passwords

- ☑ Identify customer credentials that had been compromised, and ask for additional verification of their identities before allowing transactions

- ☑ Monitor emails and login attempts to prevent the use of stolen credentials for fraud, BEC and ransomware attacks, and data breaches

But there would be some major challenges to executing that simple idea. You would need to:

☑ Collect exposed credentials frequently from many hard-to-reach sources

☑ Triage massive amounts of data to find the exposed credentials that represent real threats to your enterprise

☑ Make the database of stolen identities easy to use for both human security professionals and automated authentication and security tools

Let's see what is involved.

Sources for Stolen Identities

Exposed credentials are available from many open source, dark web, and technical sources. These include:

☑ Public and hacker databases of exposed credentials

☑ Dark web forums and marketplaces

☑ Internet relay chatrooms and social media platforms

☑ Code repositories like GitHub and paste sites like Pastebin

Creating a complete database of exposed credentials requires continually collecting updates and new posts from these sources, including invitation-only forums and marketplaces on the dark web.

ON THE WEB

Own goal! GitHub is widely used by software engineers to share software code, documentation, and other working files. Unfortunately, these sometimes contain passwords, secret keys, API tokens, and other security goodies. GitHub repositories are public by default. Developers often neglect to restrict access, and bad guys scan them regularly. In this Comparitech blog post, you can read how one security team intentionally exposed a set of AWS credentials on GitHub and watched malicious hackers pounce on them literally in a minute: It takes hackers 1 minute to find and abuse credentials exposed on GitHub (https://www.comparitech.com/blog/information-security/github-honeypot/).

High-Volume Triage

The vast majority of exposed credentials available from open source and dark web sources are duplicates or fakes, or do not pose a threat to your enterprise. Sorting through them all is a massive task. What needs to be pruned?

Duplicates and fakes

Most analysts estimate that two-thirds or more of the entries in databases of exposed credentials are duplicates. Often the same entries appear three, four, or many more times because:

☑ The same credentials may have been compromised in multiple data breaches or phishing attacks

☑ Databases and lists of credentials for sale copy from each other

The bad actors who sell stolen information aren't scrupulous about copying and reselling each other's data. Not only that, they sometimes bulk up their lists by creating fake users with email addresses from popular domains. So much for honor among thieves.

Non-threatening threats

Suppose you find an entry with the correct email address for one of your employees (jane.smith@mycompany.com) and a password, "genius1." Are you exposed? Not if your organization has been enforcing a password policy that requires a minimum of eight characters, or the use of at least one capital letter or one special character. Jane Smith was probably using her business email address and "genius1" for a website or social media account that was hacked, but you know that she must have a different password for her company login.

Outdated credentials

There are other types of credentials that don't represent a meaningful threat, for example, the credentials of:

- ☑ People who have changed their passwords recently because they were alerted to a breach, or were forced to by your organization's access policies, or are just security minded
- ☑ People who no longer work for the enterprise (assuming you disable accounts when people leave)
- ☑ Customers whose accounts have been terminated

Clearly we need automated tools for filtering and triage to avoid spending most of our time on duplicates, fakes, non-threats, and problems that have already fixed themselves.

Do Hashed Passwords Get a Pass?

A significant number of stolen passwords are hashed (encoded by a one-way transformation) prior to storage. Does that mean they're secure? Not necessarily. A password (say, Qwerty123) transformed by a specific hash algorithm (say, MD5) will always have the same hash value (in this case, 2AF9B1BA42D-C5EB01743E6B3759B6E4B).

Attackers use tables of the hash values of common passwords to put those passwords back in their original form. So a hashed version of "!!A1ntl$martXO%%^" is probably safe, but a hashed "Qwerty123" definitely is not. Hashed passwords may be a lower priority than clear ones, but they shouldn't be ignored.

Using Identity Information

There are several ways you can use identity data to prevent fraud and data breaches and improve security controls.

Scanning user accounts

An organization can take advantage of real-time collection of identity information by scanning user accounts to find and change compromised credentials.

Special vigilance can be applied to the riskiest users:

- ☑ Executives and board members

- ☑ IT systems administrators, security professionals, and others with extensive account privileges and permissions

- ☑ Managers in the treasury and finance functions and others with the power to transfer funds

- ☑ Business partners and suppliers who have credentials to access the organization's applications

- ☑ Key customers

- ☑ Users of all kinds whose credentials have been compromised most often

TIP Don't just monitor credentials for real people. Cybercriminals also value passwords associated with role-based email addresses. Search for compromised credentials that include addresses with words related to finance, administration, and supply chain management such as "invoice, "payments," "admin," "support," and "partners."

Of course, finding compromised credentials should trigger password reset requests. But you can go farther for high-risk and frequently compromised users by requiring:

- ☑ Stronger passwords

- ☑ More frequent passwords resets

- ☑ The use of MFA to access critical applications

MFA Is Not a Panacea

Multifactor authentication (MFA) is a valuable technique for protecting high-risk accounts, but it is not a panacea. In some situations, organizations are not willing to impose on users the inconveniences of setting up and using MFA. In addition, threat actors can circumvent MFA through:

- SIM swapping – convincing a mobile phone service provider to transfer a mobile account from the user's SIM card (and smartphone) to another controlled by the attacker.

- Real-time phishing – a Man in the Middle technique that uses an email link to send a user to a website controlled by the attacker where the user submits a form to a legitimate website, which returns a one-time password into the hands of the attacker, who can then use it to log in and take over the account.

- Malicious browser extensions – spyware that monitors MFA sessions between the browser and the server and captures information on the additional authentication factors.

MFA is still an important best practice, but it does not eliminate the need for additional defenses such as risk checks against compromised credentials.

Performing automatic risk checks

You can perform automatic checks for compromised credentials during critical events such as password creations and resets. Depending on the policies and culture of your organization, this could involve changing passwords automatically or informing users and asking them to make the change (perhaps within a time limit).

TIP

Use this as an opportunity to educate users. Give them a clear explanation of what happened and remind them of the importance of not using their business email address or password for social media, retail, entertainment, or other non-business accounts.

Monitoring emails and logins

Email security products often capture email addresses and passwords contained in incoming emails. Authentication tools evaluate entries from people (and bots) attempting to log onto applications. In both cases, these solutions can be integrated with an identity intelligence database to flag compromised credentials and prevent the initial stages of online fraud campaigns, BEC and ransomware attacks, and data breaches.

Determining root causes

Analyzing the incidence of compromised credentials in your user base can help you uncover systemic issues such as:

- ☑ The use of weak and common passwords that are susceptible to brute force attacks
- ☑ Supply chain partners and other third parties with poor security controls
- ☑ Business units or geographical regions particularly susceptible to credential loss

This type of analysis may highlight the need to take actions such as:

- ☑ Strengthening password policies in certain areas or globally
- ☑ Tightening access controls for third parties
- ☑ Salting and hashing stored passwords
- ☑ Increasing the use of multifactor authentication

Identity Intelligence as a Service

Identity intelligence is a specialized field. Most enterprises will want to investigate identity intelligence service offerings rather than building their own capabilities. A service provider should be able to offer identity intelligence with:

- Real-time collection of identity information
- Wide coverage of open source, dark web, and technical sources

- Efficient and accurate triaging of data to eliminate duplicates, fakes, and credentials that are not threats to your organization
- Automatic lookups of exposed credentials
- Tools to query and analyze data for individual users, batches of users, and entire business units

Chapter 14

Attack Surface Intelligence

In this chapter

- Learn what comprises an organization's digital attack surface
- Explore how attack surface intelligence services discover unknown domains and exposed internet-facing assets
- Understand how many groups inside and outside of IT can use attack surface intelligence

Your Digital Attack Surface Is Bigger Than You Think

Today, most medium-sized organizations have hundreds of internet-facing assets that are potentially susceptible to attack. Large enterprises have thousands. And very few organizations can identify, much less monitor, the majority.

Sure, most businesses and government agencies have only a few top-level domains (e.g., www.recordedfuture.com) and maybe a few dozen subdomains (blog.recordedfuture.com, support.recordedfuture.com, etc.). But how many assets have an IP address and connect to the internet? Add up:

☑ Every laptop, desktop computer, and mobile device used by employees

☑ Each server, network device, security appliance, and networked printer in every data center and office

☑ All the virtual servers, databases, services, and other workloads on cloud platforms

☑ The entire inventory of web-connected sensors, cameras, robots, and other IoT devices

The majority of these are protected by some type of firewall or access control system. But some are not, and it only takes one or a few exposed systems to give attackers an avenue into an organization.

Attack surface intelligence is information about networks and systems that can be accessed over the internet and the risks they create. Attack surface intelligence solutions and services help security teams:

☑ Discover all the organization's internet-facing assets

☑ Analyze the exposed assets to determine which ones are most likely to have vulnerabilities or security issues

☑ Continuously monitor the organization's attack surface to detect new domains and assets that might create risks

Hidden Risks

How can security teams not know about internet-facing assets or not be aware of serious security issues? Typical causes include:

- Abandoned application development projects and marketing demonstration environments that leave in place unused domains and subdomains

- Forgotten domains and assets belonging to acquired entities

- "Shadow IT" systems and cloud application subscriptions outside the organization's security controls

- Server misconfigurations such as open ports that allow unauthorized access to internal networks

- Hostnames and self-signed certificates that point to internal IP addresses

- Cloud hosting services missing controls needed for security or regulatory compliance

Discovering Internet-Facing Assets

The first task of an attack surface intelligence service or solution is to discover all of an organization's assets that could potentially be exploited by threat actors. This process involves checking a variety of databases and third-party sources and running scans on the internet.

The discovery process includes:

- ☑ Checking domain registries and the WHOIS database for all top-level domains and subdomains associated with the organization
- ☑ Conducting reverse DNS searches to discover all the IP addresses pointed to by the domains and subdomains
- ☑ Checking regional internet registries (RIRs) to find all the IP addresses registered to the organization
- ☑ Finding self-signed certificates with pointers to internal IP addresses

The data can then be used to create an inventory of the organization's entire domain portfolio and all the IP addresses that could be reached from outside.

 Don't be surprised if the discovery process yields hundreds or even thousands of previously unknown domains, subdomains, and internet-connected systems. That's a typical, if rather sobering, result. Use the findings to determine and address root causes such as carelessness on the part of application development or marketing groups, shadow IT activities, inadequate vetting of the IT systems of acquired organizations, and incomplete monitoring of cloud environments.

Discovery can also find subdomain takeovers.

Subdomain Takeovers

Sometimes an organization registers a subdomain and never uses it, or uses the subdomain for a time and then removes the host providing content to it.

Those situations give malicious actors an opening to take control of the subdomain by contacting the hosting service and connecting their own virtual host. An attacker then may be able to:

- Send phishing emails that appear to come from the organization's top level domain

- Post controversial or embarrassing content to the subdomain ("defacement")

- Execute cross-site scripting (XSS) and cross-site request forgery (CSRF) attacks

Subdomain takeovers can be used to mislead customers and employees in much the same way as "lookalike domains." If www.avaliddomain.com is the website of a legitimate business, how could a user know that a form on freegift.avaliddomain.com or an email from support.avaliddomain.com are part of a fraud campaign?

Analyzing the Exposed Assets

After creating an inventory of internet-facing assets, an attack surface intelligence service or solution can acquire information from those assets, analyze the information, and list the assets most likely to have vulnerabilities or security issues.

Potential vulnerabilities

One typical problem is servers with misconfigurations, such as open ports and remote access parameters that might allow malicious parties to gain unauthorized access to networks and applications.

Another area of concern is outward-facing systems with software tools and applications known to be frequently targeted by threat actors. Examples include websites with a contact management system (CMS), ecommerce platforms, database servers, and JavaScript libraries.

An attack surface intelligence solution can also parse DNS records and SSL certificates to see if they point to internal infrastructure and IP addresses of internal systems that could be exploited by attackers.

Policy violations

An attack surface intelligence solution can identify systems that might violate company policies, such as systems that should be – but aren't – protected by special security controls. An example is a system that handles credit card information but is outside an organization's designated cardholder data environment (CDE). Another example would be digital certificates registered with a free certificate authority when that violates the organization's security policy.

Policy violations can also occur when workloads are running on cloud hosting platforms that do not provide all the security controls needed to comply with stringent regulatory requirements such as the GDPR and some of the high-level NIST standards.

Defenses in place

On the other side of the coin, an analysis can also show which systems are protected by defenses such as web application firewalls (WAFs). This information is handy because such systems can be assigned a lower priority for remediation than equivalent ones that are more exposed.

TECH TALK

Attack surface intelligence solutions do not replace vulnerability scanners, but rather complement them. When the solution discovers and analyzes all internet-facing assets, an organization can focus vulnerability scanning efforts on the highest-risk applications and systems.

Continuously Monitoring the Attack Surface

Today, digital attack surfaces evolve and transform at a rapid rate. Organizations continually expand their web presence with new marketing, ecommerce, order tracking, customer support, supply chain, social media, and other web projects. Dynamic cloud applications frequently create and move application workloads. Hundreds of new devices with IP addresses can be brought online at any time. These activities create conditions for new security issues to emerge, often in areas invisible to conventional security tools.

Attack surface intelligence solutions can help organizations stay on top of the situation by monitoring these changes and highlighting affected assets that need to be investigated, such as:

- ☑ Newly registered domains and subdomains associated with the organization and its brands
- ☑ New servers and systems with high-risk software
- ☑ Systems belonging to acquisition targets and third-party partners with misconfigurations and policy violations

With attack surface intelligence, security teams can work with a dynamic inventory of web-facing assets, instead of static, outdated lists of IP addresses.

Who Uses Attack Surface Intelligence?

Attack surface intelligence is valuable for quite a few groups inside and outside of IT. It can help:

- ☑ Vulnerability management teams prioritize patching, identify assets affected by new CVEs, and start covering previously unknown assets
- ☑ SOC teams enrich alerts with attack surface data and prioritize the remediation of high-risk assets
- ☑ Incident response, threat hunting, and forensics teams obtain a hacker's view of the organization's entire digital attack surface, including unknown and forgotten domains, high-risk assets, and internal IP addresses exposed by DNS records and digital certificates
- ☑ Compliance and third-party risk management teams identify policy violations and pinpoint weaknesses in the IT environments of third parties and acquisition prospects
- ☑ Security analysts reduce attack surfaces by identifying and eliminating or mitigating the root causes of exposed internet-facing assets

In short, attack surface intelligence not only helps security teams be more efficient and effective, it can support corporate initiatives for digital transformation, policy compliance, and third-party risk management.

Chapter 15

Intelligence for Security Leaders

- See how intelligence supports risk management and investments in security programs
- Explore the types of intelligence CISOs find most valuable
- Review how intelligence mitigates the security skills gap

The job of the CISO has seen dramatic shifts in recent years. It once centered on making decisions about purchasing and implementing security technologies. Now, CISOs are far more likely to interact with the CEO and the board and to perform delicate balancing acts of pre-empting risk while ensuring business continuity.

Security leaders need to be able to:

☑ Assess business and technical risks, including emerging threats and "known unknowns," that might impact the business

☑ Identify the right strategies and technologies to mitigate risks

☑ Communicate the nature of risks to top management and justify security investments based on financial value to the business

Intelligence is a critical resource for all of these activities.

Risk Management

Perhaps the greatest responsibility of the modern CISO is risk management. This involves allocating resources and budget to minimize the likely impact of threats on the business. Figure 15-1 outlines the stages security leaders often move through when approaching this challenge.

Assess Security Requirements	Understand business and IT objectives and define responsibilities for the security function.
Assess Existing Security Protocols	Analyze current security people, processes, and technologies to develop an accurate picture of the security function.
Develop Initiatives	Use a risk-based approach to identify the most significant gaps in security, then define and prioritize initiatives to address them.
Track Progress	Continually monitor progress and ensure the security function is improving in line with requirements. Develop metrics to measure ongoing effectiveness.

Figure 15-1: A standard approach to assessing risk and developing a security strategy. (Source: Recorded Future)

Internal data is not enough

The approach to security outlined in Figure 15-1 is dependent on having good intelligence about relevant risk factors and potential weaknesses in existing security programs. However, too often this kind of intelligence is only gathered from internal audits, known issues, and previous security incidents. That approach produces a list of challenges that have already affected your organization, but leaves out challenges that are on the horizon and haven't yet reached you.

External context is necessary to:

- ☑ Verify risk that's related to known problems

- ☑ Warn about emerging and unforeseen threats

Internal network traffic data, event logs, and alerting obviously bring value to risk management, but they don't provide enough context to build a comprehensive risk profile — and certainly not enough to define an entire strategy. Security professionals must be proactive about uncovering unknown risks. Context is what enables security leaders to determine which potential threats are most likely to become actual threats to their organization.

Sharpening the focus

Intelligence provides context on general trends such as:

- ☑ The types of attacks that are becoming more (or less) frequent

- ☑ The types of attacks that are most costly to victims

- ☑ TTPs of new threat actors who are coming forward, and the assets and organizations they are targeting

- ☑ The security practices and technologies that have proven the most (or least) successful in stopping or mitigating these attacks

Data and information on these trends allow security organizations to anticipate which threats will be the hot news items of tomorrow. However, contextualized external intelligence is much more powerful. For example, it enables security groups to assess whether an emerging threat is *likely* to affect their specific organization based on factors like:

- ☑ **Industry**: Is the threat affecting other businesses in our vertical?

- ☑ **Technology**: Does the threat involve compromising software, hardware, or other technologies used in our organization?

☑ **Geography:** Does the threat target facilities in regions where we operate?

☑ **Attack method:** Have techniques used in the attack (including social engineering and technical methods) been used successfully against our organization or similar ones?

Without a depth of intelligence gathered from an extremely broad set of external data sources, it is impossible for security decision-makers to gain a holistic view of the cyber risk landscape and identify the greatest risks to their organization.

Figure 15-2 illustrates how a customized intelligence dashboard highlights intelligence that is most relevant to a specific organization.

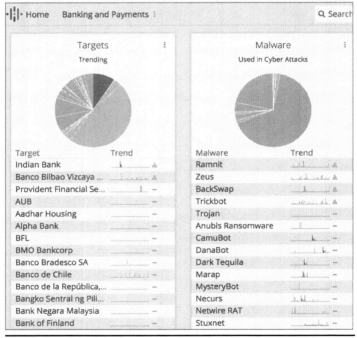

Figure 15-2: An intelligence dashboard pinpoints threats most relevant to a specific industry or technology. (Source: Recorded Future)

Mitigation: People, Processes, and Tools

Vulnerability scans and techniques such as penetration testing and red teaming contribute to a security team's ability to understand where gaps exist in their defenses. However, many organizations have far more process vulnerabilities and more weaknesses in their security practices and policies than they can fix in the short term.

Intelligence enables security leaders to pinpoint the challenges that need to be addressed first by indicating:

☑ The threat actors most likely to target the organization

☑ The TTPs those threat actors use, and the weaknesses they tend to exploit

Early warnings

Analysts find threat actors on the dark web discussing or advertising malware targeting your technology stack. Sometimes these threat actors use these platforms to recruit like-minded coders to assist them.When monitoring dark web forums and marketplaces, analysts are also able to track the development and sale of malware targeting specific vulnerabilities and other malicious tools.

Intelligence connects the dots across all of these entities to provide context on what they mean to your organization. And, as discussed earlier in this book, it is critical to focus on patching the vulnerabilities and mitigating the weaknesses that are actually at risk of being exploited before tackling others where exploitation is merely theoretical.

 TIP

Use an intelligence solution to scan the dark web and other sources for references to your organization, your industry, and specific technologies installed in your organization.

Investment

Deciding how to invest in cybersecurity has become a daunting challenge in recent times. Financial investment advisers Momentum Partners identified more than 3,500 companies in 2021 that specialize in cybersecurity technologies and services. With so many choices, how are CISOs supposed to identify the most effective solutions to implement as part of a proactive security strategy?

The only logical way is to make investment decisions based on risk. Each organization has its own unique risk profile, shaped by its industry, physical locations, and internal infrastructure. Intelligence enables security leaders to understand the most pressing threats to their organization, making the tasks of identifying and justifying areas for investment much simpler. The end goal is to be able to judge that risk and make investments based upon sound knowledge of the threat landscape.

Communication

CISOs are often challenged by the need to describe threats and justify countermeasures in terms that will motivate non-technical business leaders, such as cost, ROI, impact on customers, and competitive advantages.

Bombarding senior stakeholders with news about every single threat is not a good option. Instead, intelligence provides powerful insights for guiding these types of discussions, such as:

- ☑ The impacts of similar attacks on companies in the same industry, and on organizations of the same size in other industries

- ☑ Cyber trends and intelligence indicating that the organization is likely to be targeted and how much loss can be expected per incident

Case Study: Intelligence and Automation at a Global Retailer

With nearly 3,600 stores and over 135,000 employees worldwide, one global retail chain faces challenges that run the gamut from loss and fraud prevention and corporate security to protecting customers' PII.

The retailer uses automation to centralize and customize intelligence for every security function. Automation ensures that the real-time intelligence going into its SIEM is accurate and highly contextual — and that the output is presented in flexible, easy-to-use formats.

The company's biggest return on investment — and the biggest advantage to managing intelligence through an all-in-one platform — is better relationships both across the cybersecurity teams and with other departments.

Says a senior manager at the company's cyber defense center: "None of us is operating in a silo. If we can use intelligence to keep us safe, but also help our program visibility, that helps to make a business case for more capabilities. Having champions on other teams to back the benefits of intelligence really helps our return on investment."

For more examples of how Recorded Future saves costs, increases productivity, and improves security, read Forrester's report: "The Total Economic Impact™ Of Recorded Future Intelligence Platform" (https://go.recordedfuture.com/forrester-tei)

Supporting Security Leaders

We have mentioned several times that intelligence for security teams needs to be comprehensive, relevant, and contextualized to be useful to members of the security organization. When it comes to CISOs and other security leaders, it also needs to be concise and timely.

For example, intelligence provides security leaders with a real-time picture of the latest threats, trends, and events. A user-friendly intelligence dashboard (or some other "at-a-glance" format) enables security leaders to respond to a threat or communicate the potential impact of a new threat type to business leaders and board members.

DON'T FORGET Intelligence is not just for SecOps teams and threat analysts. Security leaders are also key consumers of intelligence. Think through the kinds of intelligence security leaders need on a daily basis (e.g., a dashboard and a list of key new intelligence findings from the previous day), at regular intervals (e.g., summaries and trends for a quarterly risk report), and for crises (e.g., intelligence about attacks that have just been detected), and make sure processes and intelligence tools are in place to address all of these needs.

The Security Skills Gap

One of the responsibilities of a CISO is to make sure the security and IT organization is staffed with the right people to carry out its mission. Yet, the cybersecurity field has a widely publicized skills shortage, and existing security staff frequently find themselves under the pressure of unmanageable workloads.

Intelligence provides a partial answer by automating the most labor-intensive, but critical, tasks in cybersecurity, which frees up people's time for the skill-intensive tasks for which they're trained. For example, intelligence helps prioritize the massive volume of alerts generated by SIEMs and other security tools, rapidly collects and correlates context from multiple sources, and provides the intelligence required to understand risks.

Making intelligence available across all security functions saves a huge amount of time, as security operations and incident response teams, threat analysts, vulnerability management specialists, and other security personnel are provided the intelligence and context they need to make fast, confident decisions.

Powerful intelligence also empowers more junior personnel to quickly upskill and perform above their experience level, so the CISO doesn't have to recruit as many senior practitioners.

Risk-Based Cybersecurity: A Better Way to Manage

Many security teams are either threat driven or compliance driven. Threat-driven teams are focused on reacting to the latest high-profile threats — whether or not they pose an actual risk to the organization. Meanwhile, compliance-driven teams excel at checking the boxes of compliance standards and frameworks.

Neither of these maximize security, and both make it hard to have meaningful discussions with managers and executives who are far more interested in profit and loss than threats and compliance.

In his book, "The Risk Business, What CISOs Need to Know About Risk-Based Cybersecurity," Levi Gundert offers a better alternative. His concept, called "risk-based cybersecurity," posits that:

- Risk is the possibility that an event will eventually lead to reduced profitability.

- The risk of a cyber threat is quantifiable in monetary terms with relatively little effort.

- The net impact of mitigation activities are able to be calculated by comparing the cost of mitigation with the expected savings from mitigating the risk.

- These calculations enable security programs to select the activities that maximize positive impact on the profitability of the organization.

Did a flashing yellow warning light go off in your head at the words "with relatively little effort" in point number 2? Building on the work of Douglas W. Hubbard and Richard Seiersen, Gundert illustrates how to use estimation, simulation, and a Threat Category Risk (TCR) framework to easily quantify threats to an organization in monetary terms.

Beyond guiding security teams to the most effective allocation of resources and staff, risk-based security enables security leaders to communicate with executives in a language they understand and appreciate: The language of dollars and cents.

"The Risk Business, What CISOs Need to Know About Risk-Based Cybersecurity" is available for download at https://go.recordedfuture.com/the-risk-business. For additional information on how to quantify cybersecurity risk, read Hubbard's and Seiersen's book "How to Measure Anything in Cybersecurity Risk."

Chapter 16

Intelligence for Prioritizing Emerging Threats

In this chapter

- Understand how tracking attack life cycles helps organizations anticipate and prioritize emerging threats
- Learn about three threats to watch: deepfakes, recruiting insiders, and new ways to sell databases and network access

Planning for Next Year Today

Much of this handbook discusses how intelligence enables us to detect and prevent today's attacks and prepare for those coming in the next few months. But intelligence can also play a unique role alerting us to threats that may not fully emerge until next year or the following one.

Intelligence about emerging and future threats is vital when mitigation strategies take months or years to implement fully. Preparing for a new threat type often requires learning and testing new security technologies, developing new processes for detection and response, and training security teams and employees to recognize new indicators. An early start can make the difference between being ready in advance and scrambling to catch up, or worse, becoming one of the early victims.

In this chapter we discuss how intelligence can help organizations anticipate and prioritize future threats. We then look at three examples of emerging threats and what intelligence can tell us about them today:

- ☑ Deepfakes

- ☑ Insider recruitment for fraud

- ☑ New ways of offering for sale compromised databases and network access

Using Attack Life Cycles to Assess Risks

Every attack type has a life cycle, or more accurately, a series of connected life cycles.

Technology life cycles

The technologies and tools used by attackers progress from theories, to proofs-of concepts, to implementations that are functional but difficult to use, to packages with ease of use features that can be used by people with limited skills. Over time, tools are enhanced and automated to challenge evolving defenses.

Ecosystem life cycles

Most attack types are introduced and first employed by individuals, but over time specialization increases. Different threat actors specialize in areas like:

- ☑ Creating and enhancing tools for use in attacks

- ☑ Providing infrastructure to launch attacks

- ☑ Launching and managing attacks through their life cycle (think customer support)

- ☑ Processing payments for ransomware attacks and extortion

- ☑ Selling stolen credit card and social security numbers, login credentials, and intellectual property to cyber-criminals and other buyers

Today, tools, infrastructure, and even the management of attacks can be obtained "as a service" at a low cost for a specified time period or project.

Generally speaking, the more advanced and specialized the commercial ecosystem developed for an attack type, the more widespread its use.

Targeting life cycles

Many attacks start by targeting one type of organization, product vulnerability, or geographical region. Over time they spread to larger or smaller enterprises, new industries, and more geographical regions and language speakers. Analysts can sometimes observe the expansion taking place and anticipate the next set of targets.

The advantages of tracking attack life cycles

It is possible to track malicious tools, attacker trends, and targeting life cycles in dark web and underground forum sources. Commoditized malicious tools are often discussed, shared, and sold. Threat actors exchange information about techniques and targets and recruit partners. As attack ecosystems evolve, analysts can observe the products, services, and information being offered, their prices, and their sources. As the participants in those ecosystems advertise or request services, analysts can monitor threat actor's interests to understand their plans and activities, often well before these are made public by the victims or the media.

This intelligence can help organizations identify emerging attack types well in advance, so they can get a head start on defensive technology, processes, and training. Those with larger budgets can even simulate the attacks to hone their defenses.

Let's look at some examples of emerging threats that are relevant today.

TIP Tracking attack life cycles is also a good way of avoiding unnecessary boardroom anxiety. The media is full of stories of threats that may be "emerging" for years, or never materialize. Organizations can use intelligence to correctly prioritize risks and calm managers reacting to the latest media scare.

Deepfakes: Fraud's Next Frontier

Deepfakes are images and recordings digitally altered with machine learning algorithms to present a known person doing or saying something they did not do or say.

Technologies to create deepfakes are becoming commoditized, and tools are widely available for amateur and "recreational" purposes. The primary uses so far have been attaching people's faces (celebrities, friends, and enemies) to other people's bodies (usually naked).

However, there has been a great deal of attention in the press to the potential for deepfake technology to be used in political disinformation campaigns. Indeed, there have been cases in Malaysia and Gabon where this appears to have happened (links to reports about these incidents and others mentioned in this section are included in the report listed in the "On the Web" section below).

A future threat to consumers and businesses?

But will deepfake technology be adopted by cybercriminals targeting consumers and businesses? Can intelligence tell organizations whether they are justified in starting to prepare now for countering deepfakes?

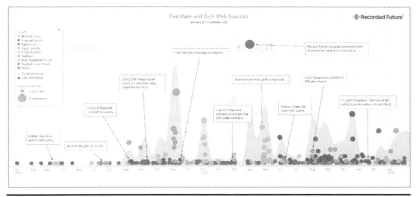

Figure 16-1: References to deepfake activities across dark web sources. (Source: Recorded Future)

Figure 16-1 shows that references to deepfake activities have picked up significantly over the past two years, including discussions about using deepfake technology for fraud campaigns. The main locations of these discussions were on English- and Russian-language deep web sites, although the topics were also raised on Turkish-, Spanish- and Chinese-language forums.

Activities have started to move well beyond the discussion phase. An increasing number of tools and services are being offered on dark web forums and marketplaces, including increasingly powerful tools to create "swap" faces and manipulate deepfake photos, videos, and audio recordings. Further, an increasing number of forums are popping up to share techniques and experiences creating advanced deepfakes, and in some cases, using them in unethical ways.

Threat actors have started offering and requesting services such as:

- ☑ Training sessions on how to create deepfakes

- ☑ Deepfake video and image creation and editing services

- ☑ Services to create fraudulent bank cards and documents using deepfake technology

Finally, a few examples of fraud perpetrated with deepfake technology have emerged. The CEO of a UK-based energy firm received a series of three phone calls from what sounded like the chief executive of his firm's German parent company with orders to transfer 220 thousand euros to the bank account of a supplier. A bank manager in Hong Kong received a phone call apparently from a company director he'd spoken with before, asking him to transfer $35 million needed for an acquisition. In fact, both were carefully prepared audio deepfakes.

So what does intelligence tell us about deepfakes as an emerging threat, and how organizations should respond?

☑ Deepfake technologies and commercial ecosystems are maturing at a rate that makes fraud-related deepfake activities a threat to businesses that needs to be taken very seriously.

☑ Organizations should start preparing mitigation strategies, such as training key employees to recognize deepfakes (at least less sophisticated ones), removing audio only authentication for important business decisions, and deploying deepfake detection technologies.

☑ Organizations should monitor the deep web for signs that deepfake technologies and ecosystems are being adapted to perform tasks such as defeating authentication methods based on face and voice recognition, or creating more convincing synthetic content for spearphishing and social engineering attacks. These would represent serious threats to existing security practices and merit an accelerated deployment of countermeasures.

ON THE WEB For an in-depth discussion of the emergence and development of deepfake activities on the dark web, read the report by the Insikt Group of Recorded Future: The Business of Fraud: Deepfakes, Fraud's Next Frontier.

Insider Recruitment for Fraud

Insider attacks have long been an important issue for security organizations, but the concern has usually been employees with a real or perceived grievance against their employer, or else departing employees taking customer lists, product designs, and other proprietary information to new employers.

Unfortunately, a new front has opened up in the war between cybercriminals and security groups: online recruitment of insiders willing to betray their employers.

The most prominent example to come to light so far was the recruitment of a Tesla employee via WhatsApp. He was offered $1 million worth of bitcoins to place malware on the company's network, malware designed to steal data from Tesla's massive "Gigafactory" in Nevada. The group behind the attack planned to demand a large ransom to refrain from leaking the auto manufacturer's proprietary information.

The employee was arrested before the scheme could be carried out, but his recruiter indicated that the criminal group had allegedly already completed several "special projects" against other companies.

Other cybercriminals have solicited insiders. The LockBit ransomware group had the inspiration (and nerve) to place an advertisement on the screens of systems they had locked down with ransomware, where it could be read by the employees of the victim and security consultants brought in to deal with the attack (see text box).

Excerpts From the LockBit Message Recruiting Insiders

Would you like to earn millions of dollars?

Our company acquire access to networks of various companies, as well as insider information that can help you steal the most valuable data of any company.

You can provide us accounting data for the access to any company, for example, login and password to RDP, VPN, corporate email, etc.

Companies pay us the foreclosure for the decryption of files and prevention of data leak.

These activities bring the issue of insider attacks to a whole new level. It is one thing to detect a few disgruntled and job-hopping employees who depend on their own, usually limited technical knowledge, to gain a small measure of revenge on their employer or favor with a new firm. It is another to have a sophisticated criminal gang dangling millions of dollars in front of the entire workforce.

Fortunately, intelligence can greatly improve the odds of detecting and blocking the solicitation of insiders by:

☑ Alerting organizations that insider recruitment is a threat needs attention and a degree of prioritization

☑ Uncovering "chatter" on the dark web about plans to target certain industries, and even certain companies, for insider recruitment, and about TTPs to be used in the attacks

☑ Monitoring social media to detect advertising campaigns targeting employees in specific enterprises

Databases and Network Access for Sale

Cybercriminals have been selling stolen databases and access to specific networks for many years, but recently the marketplaces for these commodities have become more sophisticated. For example:

☑ Breached databases are being sold in parts, for example specific combinations of email addresses, passwords, financial information, and PII.

☑ Stolen databases are being shared for free on several dark web forums.

☑ Criminal groups are offering the contents of newly compromised databases on a monthly subscription basis on dark web and file-sharing platforms.

☑ The ability to access compromised networks through stolen credentials, compromised third-party software, remote desktop protocol (RDP), internet routers, PowerShell attacks, and other methods are now being sold through auctions, with starting prices, bid steps, feedback on sellers and escrow services to hold funds until transactions are complete.

One particularly worrisome example is that ransomware groups and other threat actors often purchase network access to organizations from "initial access brokers." This division of labor enables ransomware groups and others to gain access to more networks and launch more attacks than they could have managed on their own.

In many ways these innovations are good for criminals and bad for victims. However, organizations that can navigate the new marketplaces can gather intelligence that helps them identify and fix weaknesses in their defenses.

ON THE WEB

Exposed databases often contain email addresses and passwords that can provide a way into even the best-defended organizations. To see how a single compromised password could take down the largest fuel pipeline in the U.S. and lead to gasoline shortages across the East Coast, read Hackers Breached Colonial Pipeline Using Compromised Password. For a primer on new ways that cybercriminals are monetizing compromised databases and network access, read the report by the Insikt Group of Recorded Future: Database Breaches Remain the Top Cyber Threat for Organizations (https://go. recordedfuture.com/hubfs/reports/cta-2020-0521.pdf).

Keeping Up With the Dark Web Is Hard

Intelligence from the dark web is extremely valuable for security teams, but obtaining it can be very challenging. Many forums and marketplaces are accessible only by invitation, and invitations are granted only to individuals with the right background and language skills (sometimes at the level of knowledge of a specific dialect). For the good guys, it can take years of masquerading as a malicious hacker to achieve the necessary credibility.

Section 3: Creating and Scaling Your Intelligence Program

Chapter 17

Analytical Frameworks for Intelligence

Analytical intelligence frameworks provide structures for thinking about attacks and adversaries. They promote broad understanding of how attackers think, the TTPs they use, and where in an attack life cycle specific events occur. This knowledge empowers defenders to take decisive action faster and stop attackers sooner.

Frameworks also focus attention on the details that require further investigation. This attention to detail ensures that threats have been fully removed, and that measures are put in place to prevent future intrusions of the same kind.

Finally, frameworks are useful for sharing information within and across teams and organizations. They provide common grammar and syntax for explaining the details of attacks and how those details relate to each other. A shared framework makes it easier to ingest intelligence from vendors, open source forums, information sharing and analysis centers (ISACs), and other sources.

TIP

The frameworks outlined below are complementary, not competitive. You may choose to utilize any one, two, or all three of them.

The Lockheed Martin Cyber Kill Chain®

The Cyber Kill Chain®, first developed by Lockheed Martin in 2011, is one of the first and best-known of the cyber-security intelligence frameworks. It is based on the military concept of the kill chain, which breaks the structure of an attack into stages. By segmenting an attack, defenders are able to pinpoint which stage it is in and deploy appropriate countermeasures.

The Cyber Kill Chain describes seven stages of an attack:

1. Reconnaissance
2. Weaponization
3. Delivery
4. Exploitation
5. Installation
6. Command and Control
7. Actions on Objectives (sometimes referred to as exfiltration)

These stages are often laid out in a diagram similar to Figure 17-1.

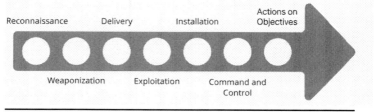

Figure 17-1: Diagram of Lockheed Martin's Cyber Kill Chain framework. (Source: Lockheed Martin)

Security teams may choose to develop standard responses for each stage.

For example, if you manage to stop an attack at the exploitation stage, you can have high confidence that nothing has been installed on the targeted systems, and full incident response activity may not be necessary.

The Cyber Kill Chain also allows organizations to build a defense-in-depth model that targets specific parts of the kill chain. For example, you might acquire intelligence specifically to monitor:

- ☑ References to your organization on the web that would indicate reconnaissance activities
- ☑ Information about weaponization against newly reported vulnerabilities in applications on your network

Limitations of the Cyber Kill Chain

The Cyber Kill Chain is a good way to start thinking about how to defend against attacks, but it has some limitations. One major criticism of this model is that it doesn't take into account the way many modern attacks work. For example, adversaries may skip reconnaissance entirely if they have no interest in targeting attacks against particular segments.

However, even with its limitations, the Cyber Kill Chain creates a solid baseline to discuss attacks and where to stop them. It also makes it easier to share information about attacks within and outside of the organization using standard, well-defined attack points.

TECH TALK Find out more about the Cyber Kill Chain by reading the seminal white paper (https://www.lockheedmartin.com/content/dam/lockheed-martin/rms/documents/cyber/LM-White-Paper-Intel-Driven-Defense.pdf)and visiting the Cyber Kill Chain website (https://www.lockheedmartin.com/en-us/capabilities/cyber/cyber-kill-chain.html).

The Diamond Model

The Diamond Model was created in 2013 by researchers at the now-defunct Center for Cyber Intelligence Analysis and Threat Research (CCIATR). It is used to track attack groups over time, rather than the progress of individual attacks.

In its simplest form, the Diamond Model looks similar to Figure 17-2. It is used to classify the different elements of an attack. The diamond for an attacker or attack group is not static — it evolves as the attacker adjusts TTPs and changes infrastructure and targets.

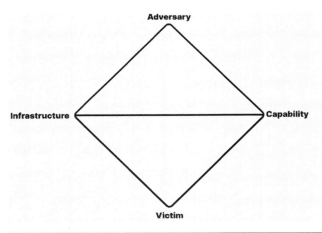

Figure 17-2: A simple Diamond Model design. (Source: CCIATR)

The Diamond Model enables defenders to track an attacker, the victims, the attacker's capabilities, and the infrastructure the attacker uses. Each of the points on the diamond is a pivot point that defenders use during an investigation to connect one aspect of an attack with the others.

Pivoting

Let's say you uncover command and control traffic to a suspicious IP address. The Diamond Model would allow you to "pivot" from this initial indicator to find information about the attacker associated with that IP address, and then research the known capabilities of that attacker. Knowing those capabilities will enable you to map adversary tools and techniques more quickly and effectively. Or, imagine that your intelligence solution uses the Diamond Model. If the board of directors asks who is launching similar attacks against other organizations in your industry (attribution), you may be able to quickly find a list of victims, the probable attacker, and a description of that attacker's TTPs. These will enable you to decide what defenses need to be put in place.

Flexibility

One of the biggest advantages of the Diamond Model is its flexibility and extensibility. You can add different aspects of an attack under the appropriate point on the diamond to create complex profiles of different attack groups. Other features of an attack that can be tracked include:

1. Phase
2. Result
3. Direction
4. Methodology
5. Resources

Drawbacks of the Diamond Model

The downside is that Diamond Models require a lot of maintenance. Some aspects of the model, especially infrastructure, change rapidly. If you don't update the diamond of an attacker constantly, you run the risk of working with outdated information. Even with these challenges, however, the Diamond Model can make the jobs of many security people easier by illustrating fast answers about evolving threats.

TIP Time stamp every update to a diamond so everybody using it has visibility into the age of the information.

TIP If you don't have the time and resources to manage this type of model yourself, you may be able to get updated information from a third-party intelligence provider.

ON THE WEB To learn more about the Diamond Model, read the Recorded Future blog post "Applying Security Intelligence to the Diamond Model of Intrusion Analysis" (https://www.record-edfuture.com/diamond-model-intrusion-analysis/), or download the original white paper "The Diamond Model of Intrusion Analysis" (https://www.activeresponse.org/wp-content/uploads/2013/07/diamond.pdf).

The MITRE ATT&CK™ Framework

MITRE is a unique organization in the United States: A corporation responsible for managing federal funding for research projects across multiple federal agencies. It has had a huge impact on the security industry, including the development and maintenance of the Common Vulnerabilities and Exposures (CVE) and the Common Weakness Enumeration (CWE) databases.

MITRE has developed a number of other frameworks that are very important for intelligence, including:

☑ The Trusted Automated Exchange of Intelligence Information (TAXII™) — a transport protocol that enables organizations to share intelligence over HTTPS and use common API commands to extract that intelligence

☑ Structured Threat Information eXpression (STIX™) — a standardized format for presenting intelligence

☑ The Cyber Observable eXpression (CybOX™) framework — a method for tracking observables from cybersecurity incidents

Categories of attacker behavior

The MITRE Adversarial Tactics, Techniques, and Common Knowledge (ATT&CK™) framework was created as a means of tracking adversarial behavior over time. ATT&CK builds on the Cyber Kill Chain, but rather than describing a single attack, it focuses on the indicators and tactics associated with specific adversaries.

ATT&CK uses 14 different tactic categories to describe adversary behavior:

1. Reconnaissance

2. Resource Development

3. Initial Access

4. Execution

5. Persistence

6. Privilege Escalation

7. Defense Evasion

8. Credential Access

9. Discovery

10. Lateral Movement

11. Collection

12. Command and Control

13. Exfiltration

14. Impact

Each of these tactical categories includes individual techniques that describe the adversary's behavior. For example, under the Initial Access category, behaviors include "Spearphishing Attachment," "Spearphishing Link," "Trusted Relationship," and "Valid Accounts."

ON THE WEB See the MITRE Enterprise ATT&CK Framework at https:// attack.mitre.org/wiki/Main_Page.

This classification of behaviors allows security teams to be very granular in describing and tracking adversarial behavior, and it makes it easy to share information between teams.

ATT&CK™ is useful across a wide range of security functions, from security operations and threat analysis to incident response. Tracking adversary behavior in a structured and repeatable way enables teams to:

☑ Prioritize incident response

☑ Map indicators to attackers

☑ Identify holes in the organization's security posture

TIP Intelligence frameworks may be used to standardize the way your security teams look at threats, indicators, vulnerabilities, and actors. If you are not prepared to build out your own framework for analysis, consider partnering with security companies that provide solutions built around existing frameworks. That approach enables you to enjoy the benefits of the framework and quickly improve the effectiveness of your security activities.

Chapter 18

Intelligence Data Sources and Types: A Framework

In this chapter

- Learn about a framework for organizing intelligence data sources and types
- See examples of data sources and types for ransomware attacks
- Review how intelligence data can guide responses to each phase of an attack

A Framework for Intelligence Data

In the previous chapter we discussed how analytical intelligence frameworks could help security teams think systematically about attacks and adversaries and examined three of them. In this chapter we present a framework developed by Recorded Future that focuses on intelligence data sources and data types that can be used to anticipate, detect, and respond to a specific threat.

The threat we use in this example is a "double extortion ransomware attack." That is an attack where adversaries exfiltrate copies of data files before encrypting the originals so they can threaten victims with the disclosure of sensitive data as well as disruption of their business. Figure 18-1 shows four stages of a double extortion ransomware attack with relevant data sources and corresponding Recorded Future data types.

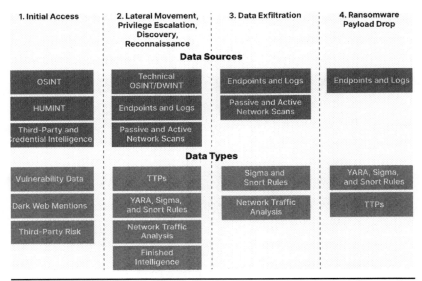

Figure 18-1: Intelligence data sources and data types for a double extortion ransomware attack. (Source: Recorded Future)

Initial Access

During the initial access phase of a double extortion ransomware attack (or any other type of ransomware attack), adversaries attempt to gain a foothold on the victim organization's network. Usually they gain access in one of these ways:

- ☑ Launching a phishing attack
- ☑ Exploiting a vulnerability on the endpoint or an internet-facing application
- ☑ Using stolen credentials

OSINT

To prevent initial access, organizations can leverage open-source intelligence (OSINT), that is, information that can be obtained on the open web and from other public sources. Probably the most important examples are vulnerability databases, published proofs of concept for existing vulnerabilities, and media reports of zero-day attacks.

HUMINT

Human intelligence (HUMINT) related to initial access includes:

- ☑ Discussions in cybersecurity forums, communities, and industry-specific Information Sharing and Analysis Centers (ISACs)
- ☑ Chatter in dark web forums
- ☑ Exploit kits and ransomware tools promoted in dark web marketplaces

This intelligence provides insight into the organizations and industries cybercriminals are targeting and the techniques and tools they are using to attack victims.

Third-party and credential intelligence

Today, cybercriminals sometimes compromise weakly defended suppliers, contractors, and other supply chain partners, then employ credentials stolen from them to gain access to their primary target. They also find or buy credentials on paste sites and dark web marketplaces. Third-party intelligence and identity intelligence can help block initial access from these avenues, as we discussed in Chapter 9 and Chapter 13.

Responses

Organizations can leverage these data sources and types to thwart initial access by:

- ☑ Monitoring email for keywords and other indicators of phishing campaigns used for ransomware attacks
- ☑ Patching the vulnerabilities that present the greatest threats to the organization
- ☑ Tightening up policies and increasing authentication requirements for high-risk users
- ☑ Scanning for attacks targeting organizations and products in your supply chain
- ☑ Monitoring the dark web for threat actors selling access to your organization and others like yours

Lateral Movement, Escalation, and Reconnaissance

During the second phase of a double extortion ransomware attack, adversaries explore the organization's network and systems, looking to expand the scope of their attack across the corporate network. If defenders detect this activity, they can work to contain the attack before any more damage is done, for example by isolating infected machines and preventing ransomware from spreading throughout the network.

Technical OSINT and DWINT

As we mentioned in Chapter 2, technical (or operational) intelligence includes information such as which vectors and vulnerabilities are used in attacks, network indicators associated with attacker command and control domains, and other cybercriminal TTPs. This type of data is available in both OSINT and dark web intelligence (DWINT) and can be enhanced by technical analysis of command and control data, malware samples, and other artifacts.

Endpoints and logs

Lateral movement, privilege escalation, discovery, and reconnaissance involve the use of open source tools, custom malware, and tools native to operating systems that can leave observable artifacts on the network, endpoints, servers, and network and security devices. Knowledge of attacker TTPs and other intelligence can direct defenders on where to look for these indicators.

Also, evidence about ongoing attacks can be found by deploying YARA, Sigma, and Snort rules to monitor endpoint systems, logs, and the network for these types of malicious behavior. These rules are signatures of malware and malicious activities at the file, log and network levels, respectively, and can be obtained from intelligence providers and cybersecurity organizations.

TECH TALK

What are YARA, Sigma, and Snort rules? YARA rules describe unique strings and byte patterns in files that security products can use to identify, classify, and block malware samples. Sigma rules are threat signatures for SIEMs. They enable SIEMs to identify log events associated with attacks such as connections to external command and control servers, account login attempts, and the use of remote access tools. Snort rules help intrusion detection and prevention systems identify scans, probes, and other malicious network-based activities. (By the way, YARA stands for "Yet Another Recursive/Ridiculous Acronym.")

Network scans

Logs can reveal much information about the intermediate stages of ransomware and other attacks, but not everything. Network scanning provides additional intelligence on vulnerabilities and attacker activity.

Passive network scanners "listen" to existing network traffic to identify the active applications, open ports, and network sessions that indicate malicious activities such as communication with external websites and unusual attempts to access sensitive data. Active scanners "talk" on networks and probe for vulnerabilities, misconfigurations, and other security weaknesses.

Honey pots are another type of passive listening technique. They catch attackers in the act of trying to navigate a fake replica of the organization's network. Honey pots provide a front-row seat to learn about attacker TTPs.

Finished intelligence

The intelligence sources and types described above can produce thousands of pieces of data in a short time. But putting those pieces together and detecting patterns requires a lot of context and background knowledge. That's why it is important to arm security and threat hunting teams with finished intelligence that describes attacks and attack methods in depth and highlights new developments and trends. Finished intelligence is available from industry organizations, government agencies, and intelligence service providers.

Responses

Organizations can use intelligence about lateral movement, privilege escalation, discovery, and reconnaissance to:

- ☑ Block network traffic to malicious IPs and URLs, such as command and control servers and websites hosting malicious tools and second-stage payloads
- ☑ Fine-tune rules and policies for SIEMs, endpoint security products, and intrusion detection and prevention systems
- ☑ Close unnecessary ports on internet-facing systems and restrict access to applications and data sources with sensitive information
- ☑ Create baselines of network and endpoint system behaviors and monitor for deviations

Data Exfiltration

Obviously, it is much better to stop a double extortion ransomware attack before any data is exfiltrated. Nevertheless, detecting attackers in the act of exfiltrating data enables organizations to:

- ☑ Cut off the data flow and limit the extent ("blast radius") of the attack
- ☑ Block or remove the ransomware payload to head off the encryption part of the attack and prevent disruption of the business

Endpoints and logs

Data exfiltration can often be detected by analyzing logs and events on endpoints. Deploying Sigma and Snort rules based on intelligence about ransomware and other threats can help SIEMs and intrusion detection and prevention products perform these tasks faster and more accurately.

Network scans

Network traffic analysis based on passive and active network scans also can help identify instances of data exfiltration, as well as network traffic to external servers and botnets used in previous ransomware attacks. Analysts can also look for unusual activities, such as the exfiltration of large amounts of data to suspicious or malicious domains and IP addresses.

Responses

When you detect data exfiltration, it is time to put your containment plan into action without delay. This process should include:

- ☑ Blocking all network traffic to and from infected machines and external websites associated with the attack
- ☑ Analyzing endpoint and log data to determine the point of initial access and what systems have been compromised
- ☑ Quarantining the compromised systems and removing malware and malicious tools, including the code used to exfiltrate data and the ransomware payload
- ☑ Determining what data has been exfiltrated and taking appropriate steps to change credentials and notify interested parties

Ransomware Payload Drop

The final phase of a double extortion ransomware attack involves dropping the ransomware payload onto endpoints and servers on the network, encrypting files, and sending ransom demands.

In some ransomware attacks all of this happens in a very short period, and the victim organization doesn't have time to contain the spread. However, in other cases the activities are spread out, and early detection can allow security teams to contain the spread.

Endpoints and logs

Most of the malicious activities in this phase of the attack occur on endpoints and servers, so early warning is best obtained by analyzing changes there. Activities associated with malware include:

☑   Accessing and modifying files at an unusual volume

☑   Disabling security tools

☑   Removing or modifying backups

☑   Interfering with processes and services that make recovery easier

As with the previous phases, intelligence embedded in YARA, Sigma, and Snort rules can play a major role enabling antimalware products, SIEMs, and intrusion detection and prevention systems to identify malicious behavior and provide intelligence that can be used post-compromise.

This is also an area where intelligence about attacker TTPs can play a vital role by giving security teams timely information on what the attackers will do next.

A Flexible Framework

This discussion has covered just one example of a framework for intelligence data sources and types. The framework will vary for other types of attacks, with fewer or more phases and different forms of intelligence. But in any attack scenario the process of creating such a framework will help your team:

☑   Identify and the best sources of intelligence for each phase of the attack, and obtain access to them

☑   Identity the most useful data types and set up tools and processes to capture, analyze, present, and disseminate key intelligence

☑   Achieve consensus on priorities for acquiring and using intelligence

Chapter 19

Your Intelligence Journey

In this chapter

- Examine ways to clarify your intelligence needs and goals
- Explore key success factors that contribute to effective programs
- Learn how to start simple and scale up

I
n this chapter, we suggest some best practices for mapping out your intelligence journey and building toward a comprehensive intelligence program.

Don't Start With Threat Feeds

Many organizations begin their intelligence programs by signing up for threat data feeds and connecting them with a SIEM solution. This may seem like a logical way to start because many threat data feeds are open source (i.e., free), and the technical indicators they deliver appear useful and easy to interpret. Since all malware is bad, and every suspicious URL could be used by an attacker, the more clues you have about them the better, right?

In reality, the vast majority of honeypot results, malware samples, and suspicious URLs are not relevant to current threats to your organization. That's why feeding large volumes of unfiltered threat data to your SIEM will almost certainly create more alerts than answers — and ultimately, the kind of alert fatigue we examined in Chapter 4.

Clarify Your Intelligence Needs and Goals

Because intelligence provides value to so many teams across your organization, it is important to develop priorities that accurately reflect the organization's overall needs and goals.

Answer these questions

Develop a clear set of goals by determining the needs of each security group in your organization and the advantages that intelligence will provide for them.

Begin by considering these questions:

- ☑ What are your greatest risks?

- ☑ In what ways do you need intelligence to address each of those risks?

- ☑ What is the potential impact of addressing each risk?

- ☑ What gaps need to be filled by information, technology, or people to make intelligence effective in those areas?

ON THE WEB For a comprehensive look at the power of intelligence, download "The Ultimate Security Intelligence Kit" (https://www.recordedfuture.com/ultimate-security-intelligence-kit/). This curated collection of white papers, reports, videos, podcasts, and more describes in detail how intelligence works and all the ways it benefits your organization.

Identify which of your teams will benefit from intelligence

Teams across your entire organization will benefit from intelligence that drives informed decision-making and provides insightful perspectives. Intelligence that is comprehensive, relevant, and easy to consume has the potential to revolutionize how different roles in your organization operate day to day. When determining how to move your intelligence strategy forward, it's important to identify all of the potential users in your organization and align the intelligence to their unique use cases. Be sure to think outside of your security organization as well, because groups like legal, HR, IT, and business operations also benefit from intelligence.

DON'T FORGET Drill down into which outputs of intelligence each group will use and exactly how they will benefit in terms of response times, cost savings, staff efficiency, investment decisions, etc. The needs and benefits are not always obvious. Documenting these details will enable you to set priorities, justify investments, and find new uses for intelligence.

Key Success Factors

There are several factors that frequently contribute to effective intelligence programs. The sooner you implement these, the faster you'll realize the full value of intelligence .

Generating quick wins with monitoring

Monitoring security information often provides quick benefits with relatively modest investments. The key is to look for a few types of data that are particularly meaningful to your business and information security strategy for anticipating emerging threats and providing early warnings of actual attacks. These activities might include:

- ☑ Checking for new vulnerabilities that affect your most important software packages, servers, and endpoints
- ☑ Tracking threat trends that pose potential risks to your business operations
- ☑ Watching for any leaked corporate credentials, data, or code appearing on public or dark web sites
- ☑ Scanning the web and social media for the names of your organization and its brands, business units, and products

There are likely a few data types of vital importance to your business that are possible to monitor without investing in new infrastructure or staff. Doing so is likely to generate quick wins, demonstrate the advantages of intelligence, and build enthusiasm for the program.

Ensuring that reports are useful

Many organizations get into the rut of producing daily reports that are of little to no use. Often these take the form of bulleted lists of detected threats with a simple low/medium/high impact rating. While these reports show that analysts are keeping busy and raising awareness of cyber threats across the organization, they typically have zero impact on operational outcomes.

Don't worry about producing reports on a schedule. Instead, make sure that every report and communication you do produce contains intelligence and insights that empower the affected parties to make decisions and take appropriate actions. Ideally, these will include at least basic information on:

- ☑ The probable threat actor(s)

- ☑ Techniques and tools used by the threat actor(s)

- ☑ Likely targets in the organization

- ☑ Whether the threat represents a real danger to the organization

- ☑ The likelihood that existing security controls are able to mitigate the threat

- ☑ Recommended actions to take in response

Automating as much as possible

Effective intelligence programs typically focus on automation from the very beginning. They start by automating fundamental tasks like data aggregation, comparison, labeling, and contextualization. When these tasks are performed by machines, humans are freed up to focus on making effective and informed decisions.

As your intelligence program becomes more sophisticated, you may find even more opportunities for automation. You will be able to automate information sharing among a larger group of security solutions and automate more workflows that provide intelligence to security operations and incident response teams, threat analysts, fraud prevention teams, vulnerability management specialists, third-party risk managers, and brand defenders. You will be able to offload more of the high-volume work to your intelligence solutions by having the software automatically correlate threat data, produce risk scores, identify false positives, and much more.

When you evaluate intelligence solutions, examine the level to which they employ automation. Is automation confined to aggregating and cross-referencing data, or does the solution add context that equips your teams to make risk-based decisions with confidence? Keep in mind that inputting more raw data into your intelligence software only adds value if it's automatically analyzed, organized, and delivered to you in an easy-to-consume format with context.

Integrating intelligence with processes and infrastructure

Integrating an intelligence solution into your existing systems is an effective way to make the intelligence accessible and usable without overwhelming teams with new technologies.

A key part of integration involves ensuring that your intelligence solution has visibility into the security events and activities captured by your existing security and network tools. Combining and correlating internal and external data points produces genuine intelligence that is both relevant to your business and placed in the context of the wider threat landscape.

The other critical aspect of integration is delivering the most important, specific, relevant, and contextualized intelligence to the right group at the right time. To accomplish this, integrate your intelligence solution with your SIEM and other security tools, either through APIs or via interfaces developed in partnership with the security tool vendors.

When you evaluate intelligence solutions, it's important to understand which ones easily integrate with your existing software and support your security teams' use cases.

Getting experts to nurture internal experts

The value you get from intelligence is directly related to your ability to make it relevant to your organization and apply it to existing and new security processes.

You will reach these goals faster if you work with a vendor or consultant that provides technical capabilities and expertise that empower your organization to get the most from intelligence. As time goes on, working with such a partner will enable members of your team to become intelligence experts in their own right.

DON'T FORGET Look for partners that have a wide and deep bench of intelligence experts. These specialists should have the knowledge and experience to understand your needs in order to assist you in realizing the most value from your investment. Be sure they will be available when you call on their expertise, and that they will work with you to identify new advantages from leveraging intelligence in your organization. Your chosen partners must be committed to your success today and continue to support your security teams as you move forward.

ON THE WEB Find more information on selecting the right intelligence solution by downloading "The Buyer's Guide to Intelligence," from Recorded Future. It includes a handy RFP template to use in evaluating the capabilities of different vendors. (https://go.recordedfuture.com/buyers-guide).

Start Simple and Scale Up

Intelligence is not a monolith that needs to be dropped onto the security organization all at one time. Instead, you have options in how you collect, process, analyze, and disseminate intelligence to various stakeholders and groups.

You may choose to start simple with your current staff (instead of building a dedicated intelligence team), a few data sources, and integration with existing security tools like your SIEM and vulnerability management system. Soon, you may benefit from scaling up with dedicated staff, more data sources, more tools integrations, and more automated workflows, as shown in Figure 19-1.

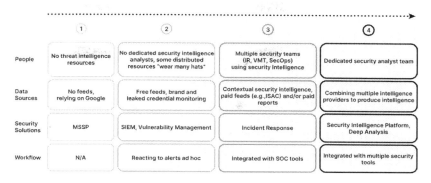

	1	2	3	4
People	No threat intelligence resources	No dedicated security intelligence analysts, some distributed resources "wear many hats"	Multiple security teams (IR, VMT, SecOps) using security intelligence	Dedicated security analyst team
Data Sources	No feeds, relying on Google	Free feeds, brand and leaked credential monitoring	Contextual security intelligence, paid feeds (e.g.,ISAC) and/or paid reports	Combining multiple intelligence providers to produce intelligence
Security Solutions	MSSP	SIEM, Vulnerability Management	Incident Response	Security Intelligence Platform, Deep Analysis
Workflow	N/A	Reacting to alerts ad hoc	Integrated with SOC tools	Integrated with multiple security tools

Figure 19-1: Four stages of intelligence program maturity — from no internal resources to a fully staffed and highly automated program. (Source: Recorded Future)

Start your journey by researching the needs of each group in your security organization and determining how intelligence will enable them to achieve their objectives.

Over time, you will be able to build toward a comprehensive intelligence program that:

- ☑ Scours the widest possible range and variety of technical, open, and dark web sources
- ☑ Uses automation to deliver easily consumable intelligence
- ☑ Provides fully contextualized alerts in real time with limited false positives
- ☑ Integrates with and enhances your other security technologies and processes
- ☑ Consistently improves the efficiency and efficacy of your entire security organization

Chapter 20

Developing Your Core Intelligence Team

In this chapter

- Understand the processes, people, and technology that make up a dedicated intelligence capability
- Learn how these teams use intelligence to judge risk and drive business continuity
- Review ways to engage with intelligence communities

We have seen how intelligence benefits your security teams. Now here are a few suggestions about how to organize your core team dedicated to intelligence.

Dedicated, but Not Necessarily Separate

As we discussed in the previous chapter, you may want to start your intelligence journey with people who continue to play other roles on different security teams in the organization, as well.

Eventually, two questions will likely arise:

1. Should there be a dedicated intelligence team?
2. Should it be independent, or live inside an existing security group?

The answers are: Yes, and it depends.

A dedicated team is best

As you develop a comprehensive intelligence program, you will need to build a team that's dedicated to collecting and analyzing threat data and turning it into intelligence. The sole focus of this team will be to provide relevant and actionable intelligence to key stakeholders, including senior executives and members of the board.

Dedication and a broad perspective are required to ensure your team members devote enough time to collecting, processing, analyzing, and disseminating intelligence that provides the greatest value to the organization as a whole. It's critical to avoid the temptation to focus on the intelligence needs of a single group over any other.

Where the team sits depends on your organization

Having an intelligence team with organizational independence (shown in Figure 20-1 as the SI Manager and team) has its advantages — such as greater autonomy and prestige.

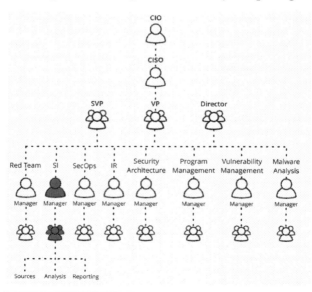

Figure 20-1: Intelligence as an independent group in the security organizational structure (shown as the SI Manager and team).

However, these advantages may be completely offset by political issues associated with creating a team with a new high-level manager and its own budget that pulls skilled analysts out of their existing groups.

A dedicated intelligence team does not necessarily need to be a separate function reporting directly to a VP or the CISO, especially when starting out. It may instead belong to a group that already works with intelligence. In many cases this will be the security operations or incident response team. Taking this approach is often a viable option to avoid conflict with entrenched security teams.

Picking the People

If you take a gradual approach to building your core intelligence team, start with individuals who are already in the security organization and are currently applying intelligence to their particular areas of expertise. They may not have the title "intelligence analyst" or see themselves that way at first, but they are likely the most capable people available to form the backbone of your emerging intelligence group. While you can hire recent graduates with cybersecurity degrees, we recommend against this approach, because networking and security experience is highly valuable to a new team, particularly at the beginning of a program.

Core Competencies

The intelligence function exists to strengthen every other security team — empowering everyone to better protect the entire organization. It is critical that the intelligence team includes people who understand the core business, operational workflows, network infrastructure, risk profiles, and the supply chain, as well as the organization's technical infrastructure and software applications.

As the intelligence team matures, you may want to add members who are skilled at:

☑ Correlating external data with internal telemetry

- ☑ Reverse engineering malware and reconstructing attacks (forensics)
- ☑ Providing threat situational awareness and recommendations for security controls
- ☑ Proactively hunting internal threats, including insider threats
- ☑ Data engineering and signature generation for Yara, SIGMA, or other rule sets
- ☑ Educating employees and customers about cyber threats
- ☑ Engaging with the wider intelligence community
- ☑ Identifying and managing information sources

You may also want to add staff with diverse backgrounds, including experience outside of information technology. In particular:

- ☑ **Analysts with military and intelligence backgrounds** generally understand how to structure processes for data collection, analysis, and reporting, how to adjust for biases in sources, and how to present intelligence and conclusions in ways that are clear, concise, and tailored for their audience.
- ☑ **Staff members with law enforcement experience** have knowledge about criminal tactics and methods, and are effective at distinguishing fact from opinion.

Collecting and Enriching Threat Data

We discussed data sources data in chapter 2. Here we explore how to work with a range of sources to ensure accuracy and relevance.

The human edge

Intelligence vendors often provide some types of strategic intelligence, but you may also develop in-house capabilities to gather information about the topics and events that are most relevant to your organization.

For example, you may decide to develop an internal web crawler that analyzes the web page code of the top 5,000 web destinations visited by your employees. This analysis might provide insights into the potential for drive-by download attacks. You could share the insights with the security architecture team to assist them in proposing controls that defend against those attacks. This kind of intelligence generates concrete data, which is much more useful than anecdotes, conjecture, and generic statistics about attacks.

Additional sources

Proprietary sources that may strengthen your intelligence resources include:

- ☑ Vendor or ISAC feeds
- ☑ Allow lists
- ☑ Deny lists
- ☑ Intelligence team research

Combining sources

An automated intelligence solution enables the security teams to centralize, combine, and enrich data from multiple sources — before the data is ingested by other security systems or viewed by human analysts on security operations teams.

Figure 20-2 shows the elements of such an automated threat solution. In this process, information from an intelligence vendor is filtered to find data that is important to the organization and specific security teams. Then it is enriched by data from internal intelligence sources and output in formats that are appropriate for tools including the SIEM, ticketing system, and more. This automated translation of raw data into relevant insights is the essence of intelligence.

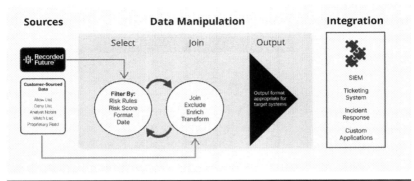

Figure 20-2: An intelligence platform centralizes, combines, and enriches data, and then formats it for multiple target systems. (Source: Recorded Future)

The role of intelligent machines

We've reached the point where automated components have successfully learned the language of threats and are able to accurately identify malicious terms.

Advances in analytics and natural language processing (NLP) bring additional advantages to the intelligence team. With the right technology, references to threats from all sources are able to be rendered language neutral. This enables humans and machines to analyze them, regardless of the original language the references appeared in.

The combination of analytics and NLP offers huge opportunities for organizations to leverage intelligence. Not only do these technologies remove language barriers, but they also have the potential to reduce analyst workloads by taking on many tasks related to data collection and correlation. When combined with the power to consider multiple data and information sources concurrently to produce genuine intelligence, these capabilities make it far easier to build a comprehensible map of the threat landscape.

Engaging With Intelligence Communities

Intelligence cannot flourish in a vacuum. External relationships are essential to successful intelligence teams. No matter how advanced your team might be, no single group is as smart as the intelligence world as a whole.

Many intelligence communities allow individual organizations to share relevant and timely attack data, enabling other members to protect their organizations before they are victimized. Engaging with trusted communities such as ISACs is crucial for decreasing risk — not just for your individual organization, but also for the entire industry and the cyber world at large. Participation requires time and resources, such as communication with peers via email and attendance at security conferences. However, relationship building must be a priority for intelligence to be successful.

Conclusion

Using Intelligence to Disrupt Adversaries

Key Takeaways From the Book

This book began with the idea that intelligence is valuable to everyone across all security functions, and beyond. Intelligence enables teams to anticipate threats, respond to attacks faster, and make better decisions to reduce risk. Throughout this book, we examined how to adopt a proactive, comprehensive approach to security by applying intelligence to several facets of your organization's security strategy.

That's what intelligence is — an approach that amplifies the effectiveness of security teams and tools by exposing unknown threats, informing better decisions, and driving a shared understanding to accelerate risk reduction across the organization. The nine pillars of SecOps intelligence, vulnerability intelligence, threat intelligence, third-party intelligence, brand intelligence, and geopolitical intelligence, along with newly-introduced fraud intelligence, identity intelligence, and attack surface intelligence, provide organizations with powerful insight into the risks they face, while streamlining the ways their teams work.

What results will you achieve when you adopt these principles?

1. You will disrupt the adversaries targeting your organization.

By identifying the adversaries that are most dangerous to your organization and understanding how they work, you will put the right defenses in place and make attackers' lives so difficult that they give up on their efforts to target you.

2. You will gain the context required to make informed decisions and take action.

By generating and consuming contextual intelligence that is timely, clear, and actionable, you will enrich your knowledge, simplify decision-making processes, and amplify the impact of all of your security solutions.

3. Your people and machines will work together to increase overall effectiveness.

Machines process and categorize raw data at extraordinary speed and scale, affording humans the time and context they need to perform intuitive, big-picture analysis. By improving human and automated workflows, intelligence will save time and money, reduce human burnout, and improve security overall.

4. Your security teams — and many others in your organization — will work smarter.

Every security team, as well as executives and colleagues across your organization — from risk management and fraud prevention to brand management and third-party risk, and beyond — will receive more relevant intelligence and less irrelevant raw data. They will be able to interact with the right intelligence at the right time, in formats that are easy to understand, through existing security and collaboration tools. They will be empowered to make better decisions, faster.

One of the great advantages of intelligence is that it enables you to scale up your program in stages. Start by improving the effectiveness of core activities in security operations, incident response, vulnerability management, and threat intelligence — or by simply building new foundations for increasingly important programs relating to third-party risk, brand protection, and geopolitical security. Either way, you will achieve measurable wins for your organization at each step. We hope this handbook has provided you with a view of intelligence's vast potential, and how to achieve it!